IGNITE YOUR FUNDRAISING

A ministryTHRIVE Production

© 2018 by John D. Leavy
All rights reserved.

Reproduction or translation of any part of this work beyond that permitted by Section 107 or 108 of the 1976 United States Copyright Act without permission of the copyright owner is unlawful. Requests for permission or further information should be emailed to: John D. Leavy at john@ministrythrive.com.

This publication is designed to provide accurate and authoritative information regarding the subject matter covered. It is sold with the understanding that the publisher or author are not engaged in rendering legal, accounting or other professional services. If legal advice or other expert assistance is required, the services of a competent professional person should be sought.

ISBN-13:
978-1987584776 (John D Leavy)

ISBN-10:
1987584775

First Printing: April 2018
Printed in the United States of America

Call to Me and I will answer you,
and tell you great and mighty things,
which you do not know.

                                      Jeremiah 33:3

Contents

THE ROADMAP
What You'll Learn, What You'll be Able to Do vii

ONE
Deciding on Your Fundraising Goals 1

TWO
Acquiring New Donors 15

THREE
Telling a Great Story 38

FOUR
Getting Your Message Out 46

FIVE
Setting Things in Motion 56

SIX
Following Up 64

SEVEN
Measuring Your Progress 78

EIGHT
Getting Better Results 94

NINE
End-of-the-year Fundraising 114

The Preface

Scan the Internet for the most common reasons fundraising efforts fail and the causes become all too obvious. The list of reasons looks a bit like this: no written plan, unreasonable expectations, lack of preparation, time, or resources, poor communication, failure to convince the potential donor of the importance of the mission, ambiguous storytelling, lack of an effective ask, and a scarcity of updates or follow up. Perhaps you could add a few more items to this list.

Ignite Your Fundraising helps you set realistic goals, tell a more effective story, help grow and target your audience, get your message out, manage all the moving parts, track and follow up on new donors, along with ways you can extend your fundraising efforts going forward. The book ends with a section on how to raise funds at year's end.

Ignite Your Fundraising makes the process of raising funds for your cause more organized, targeted and strategic, rewarding, fruitful, enjoyable—and less stressful.

Ignite Your Fundraising is written with at least three audiences in mind. First, those individuals who are fundraising for the first time and looking to raise their first $10,000. Second, organization's that have stalled out raising funds and need guidance in restarting the fundraising process. And lastly, those organizations who are raising funds on a regular basis but want to refine their fundraising methods, so their organization can grow and be more impactful.

Change Tomorrow!
John D. Leavy

Ignite Your Fundraising

The Roadmap

Anyone who wants to reach their destination safely and successfully rely on roadmaps. Roadmaps give us a starting point and they let us know the distance to our destination. The map's features and terrain represent what we'll encounter along the way. Roadmaps aid us in determining the preferred route and assist us in navigating unfamiliar territory.

Let's unfold the *Ignite Your Fundraising* roadmap. It covers the entire fundraising journey from setting realistic goals to measuring your success. With this book's help, you'll be able to successfully navigate the pitfalls and problems non-profits usually come upon when trying to reach their fundraising goals.

Chapter ONE: Deciding on Your Fundraising Goals, this first chapter starts out talking about setting realistic, practical goals that motivate the fundraising team to action. It uses the SMART (Specific, Measurable, Attainable, Relevant, Time Bound) method to set those objectives. From there the chapter talks about the importance of writing down the goals so everyone stays focused and on track.

Downloadable Resource(s):

- ✓ Project Priority Example
- ✓ Project Priority Worksheet

- ✓ SMART Goal Setting Example
- ✓ SMART Goal Setting Worksheet

Chapter TWO: Acquiring New Donors, even though some of the focus is on generating funds during the campaigns, two more important factors surface. That of building relationships with existing supporters and capturing the names of potential donors. Both aspects that may pay large dividends in the future.

Downloadable Resource(s):

- ✓ First 100 Names Worksheet
- ✓ Appointment Setting Script Example
- ✓ Appointment Setting Script Worksheet
- ✓ Information Card Example
- ✓ Donor Card Example
- ✓ Face-to-face Meeting Script Example
- ✓ Face-to-face Meeting Script Worksheet

Chapter THREE: Telling a Great Story, every great story needs a purpose and a hook to draw the reader into the story. Writers who tell first-rate stories don't wander. They strive to keep things brief. Good stories include real details and great photos. Writers need to tap into the reader's emotions and find ways to place the reader in the narrative. For non-profits, it's always a bonus to the story when the recipients being ministered to can be brought into the account.

Downloadable Resource(s):

✓ Telling a Great Story Worksheet

Chapter FOUR: Getting Your Message Out, one message does NOT suit all audiences. Strangers need to be introduced to the work being done. Prospective donors should be nudged into getting involved. Current donors and supporters need to know the importance of their continued support and how an increase in their contribution can make a significant difference. Major donors and regular supporters will likely want more information than those that donate one time. If we boil down a communication plan it's really nothing more than deciding what to say, to whom, when, and by what means. Of course, there's a goal component in that we want the communication that takes place between the organization and individuals to generate an action—preferably in the form of collecting email addresses or gifts.

Downloadable Resource(s):

✓ Sample Communication Plan by Donor Schedule

Chapter FIVE: Setting Things in Motion, staring at a blank screen trying to decide how to start the planning process can be daunting. All fundraising plans have a number of moving parts: there's the tasks to be accomplished, when they'll happen, who will be responsible, what resources and skills will be needed, along with a set of deadlines. The fundraising plan proposed in *Setting Things in Motion* outlines all the activities and what needs to be in place for a plan to be effective.

Downloadable Resource(s):

- ✓ Sample 6-month Fundraising Plan Schedule
- ✓ Sample Fundraising Plan Worksheet

Chapter SIX: Following Up, poor communication is one of the top reasons donors stop supporting a project and go elsewhere. Thanking a person for deciding to be involved is of paramount importance. Remember, it's more cost effective to keep the donors you have instead of spending time and money looking for new ones. Chapter SIX talks about the various aspects of being grateful for those that support the organization. You'll see an example and worksheet that talk about developing a Tiered "Thank You" System because all donors should not be treated the same. This chapter also outlines a follow up plan and schedule to make sure the communication between the organization and the donors stays strong.

Downloadable Resource(s):

- ✓ Tiered "Thank You" System Sample
- ✓ Tiered "Thank You" System Worksheet
- ✓ Sample Follow Up Plan by Donor
- ✓ Follow Up Plan by Donor Worksheet

Chapter SEVEN: Measuring Your Progress, the three factors that tell the real story about the success or failure of the fundraising effort are: **traffic**, **conversions**, and **average gift**. This chapter talks about tracking the numbers that mean the most when sending your message out by way of: websites, support letters, newsletters, email, social media, or face-to-face meetings.

Downloadable Resource(s):

✓ Measuring Your Progress Worksheet

Chapter EIGHT: Getting Better Results, helps you disassemble your fundraising approach into its discrete components so you can examine each one individually to see if improvements can be achieved. Or if shortcomings can be removed or replaced. Each section examined coincides with Chapter ONE through SEVEN. The series of questions are there to stimulate conversation and thought on how the fundraising activities might be made more effective.

Downloadable Resource(s):

✓ Getting Better Results Worksheet

Chapter NINE: End-of-the-year Fundraising, raising funds at the end of the year is not much different than an organization's normal yearlong fundraising effort—just on a more compressed schedule. The conversations at years-end is a great time to herald the success of the organization and layout the next year's plans. You'll find a Sample EOY Fundraising Plan Schedule and Worksheet at the end of the chapter to guide you on your way to a successful year-end campaign.

Downloadable Resource(s):

- ✓ Sample EOY Fundraising Plan Schedule
- ✓ Sample EOY Fundraising Plan Worksheet

You'll find loads of Tips, Show & Tell Worksheets, and Takeaways throughout *Ignite Your Fundraising*.

Tips: The author shares as much information and wisdom as possible in these brief pages. Tips such as, "Personalize your email salutation" helps people take advantage of what's most successful.

Show & Tell: There are dozens of examples, worksheets and spreadsheets labeled: Show & Tell—the worksheets are editable, so you'll be able to instantly apply what you've learned, modify the handouts and use them for your fundraising campaign.

Takeaways: You'll find these sections throughout the book. They help get you up to speed quickly on what practices are most effective and efficient to the related topic being discussed. Here's a sample:

6 Goal Setting Takeaways:

1. Set goals that motivate the team
2. Make sure the goals are in line with the organization's mission
3. Use the SMART method when setting your goals

4. Record the goals (on paper or in the cloud)
5. Develop an action plan to achieve the goals
6. Don't lose focus—stay on task

Ignite Your Fundraising

ONE

Deciding on Your Fundraising Goals

"You've got to be very careful if you don't know where you are going, because you might not get there." — Yogi Berra

Goals are important. They motivate us. They set our direction. They give us focus. They inspire us to do more than we believed we or God can do (Eph. 3:20). They give us a way to measure our progress. Goals also help to eliminate procrastination. Reaching goals help solve problems.

If we think about setting goals we can break the process down into these elements:

- Set goals that motivate.
- Use the SMART method when setting your goals.
- Write the goals down.

- Develop an action plan to achieve the goals.
- Stay focused—don't get sidetracked.

 **Goals obviously need to be in line with an organization's mission. The goals need to accomplish what needs to be done most.**

Set Goals That Motivate

The goals an organization sets need to inspire the team and stir their passion. The goals need to excite the team and create a sense of urgency to complete the mission set before them.

The team members need to understand what achieving the goals really mean to the recipients. Orphans will be feed, people will hear the Good News, pastors will be trained, wells will be dug, and micro businesses will spring up. People's quality of life will be raised. More people will enter God's Kingdom.

The team members need to know the reasons behind the goals being set.

Use the SMART Method When Setting Your Goals

If you're not familiar with the SMART goal setting method, it consists of five ingredients. Goals need to be: Specific, Measurable, Attainable, Relevant, and Time Bound.

Ignite Your Fundraising

Specific – A non-specific, fuzzy goal generates little or no interest as well as traction—or gifts. A pregnancy resource center might go with a plea to raise $150,000 by December 31 to save 550 babies in coming year. Their goal is simple and clearly spelled out. They're raising **$150,000** by **December 31** to **save 550 babies**.

If your project needs to support 50 orphans for the coming year and it costs $35 per child per month the tagline is obvious – **$21,000** by **December 31st** cares for **50 Orphans**.

Let's say you're building a wall around the girl's dormitory in an unsafe part of town and the construction cost is $9,000. Put together a campaign that has a goal of raising **$3,000** per month during a three-month period. People like deadlines.

Don't only ask people to donate money. People may have the funds to give. At other times, they may not be able to support the effort financially. Give people other ways to invest their time, talent and gifting. Perhaps they can be a regular volunteer, a one-time helper, or part of the fundraising committee.

Don't use dollar amounts people cannot relate to. Break the amount down so people can grasp the sum of money and how it's being spent. Everyone can relate to the cost of their morning latte, a dinner out, or the price of theater tickets.

 Be specific. Provide people with giving options.

Ignite Your Fundraising

If part of the campaign will be to acquire more email addresses of prospective donors or actual donors, then those numbers should be specific as well.

Suppose we consider these numbers:

- Increase the size of your donor list by 20%.
- Acquire the email addresses of 100 new prospective donors.
- Increase the number of donors that do direct deposit by 20%.
- Increase the number of monthly donors by 10.
- Acquire one more anchor donor.

Don't worry if the estimate is off.

If you don't have a long history to look back on, the odds are your estimate, as specific as you might think it is, may be high or low. You won't be able to tell if your estimates are misaligned until things are underway and you can gauge the rate of success in reaching those guesstimates.

 **Find a Project Priority Example and Worksheet at the end of this chapter.**

Measurable – Progress needs to be measured. When checking the roadmap, it's easy to tell when you're halfway to the destination. If the year-end goal is to raise **$30,000** over the **60 days** between

November and December, divide the total sum between the nine weeks that comprise that period. If after three weeks the fundraising effort has not raised $10,000, it will be obvious to everyone on the team that the fundraising is not on track, the goal may not be within reach, and adjustments need to be made.

Yes, it's great that more people may be liking your Facebook page or visiting the website, but are they taking an action—are they leaving their email address behind, are they donating, or joining in the venture?

 Measure cold, hard facts—not feelings.

Other than the sum of money needing to be raised, we'll cover how numbers tell the rest of the story in Chapter SEVEN, *Measuring Your Progress*.

<u>*Attainable*</u> – Goals need to be attainable. If you're setting goals for the first time, you'll have to mix a little reality and good fortune with a good guess. Ask around. Ask God. Find out what the average fundraising goal is for a project of your size? How successful were others that came before you?

You may need to raise $50,000 to get everything done on your list of projects. But, that doesn't mean you'll be able to raise the money in one round of fundraising.

Let's look at a for instance.

Suppose your fundraising efforts last year raised $20,000 and the year before $35,000 was raised. The likelihood of raising $50,000 during the current year's campaigns is most unlikely unless you plan on stepping up your fundraising activities significantly.

Let's imagine you have no history to look back on. Now how do you estimate your goal? You seek counsel, pray, and then make your best guess.

Using the same analogy, assume you want to raise $50,000 in the coming year. This year, if you raise $15,000 or $20,000 half way through year, the possibility of meeting the $50,000 goal is possibly out of reach unless things change.

 Set your goals as exact as you can, monitor their success closely and make changes when necessary if it looks like you'll fall short. Either dial the goals back or step-up the fundraising activities.

Settings goals that are not achievable only demoralize the team members. In the same vain, don't set goals where no one needs to work hard and there are few challenges.

 Always leave room for God to work.

Set realistic goals. Again, after expending 25% or 30% of the effort it will be obvious if the goals that were initially set are attainable. If your fundraising goal is off, adjust, and learn from it.

Ignite Your Fundraising

<u>Relevant</u> – It's important to remember, the fundraising goals need to be in line with your organization's overall vision and mission.

If there are disconnects between the work being done and the organization's vision and mission, donors may find it hard to financially support the group's efforts.

People have little interest in achieving goals if the objectives are not directly related to what they're passionate about.

It's easy to get off track when setting goals. At times the work can be overwhelming. What needs to be accomplished may be more than the organization can handle.

Stay true to your initial vision and mission. It's better to take on additional projects, or to expand one's purpose once a successful fundraising foundation has been put in place.

Make sure every team member buys into the fundraising objectives or disharmony and a lack of enthusiasm may be just around the corner.

<u>Time Bound</u> – Let's use the end-of-the-year for this example. Without deadlines few projects finish on time, or at all. The deadline for end-of-the-year fundraising is December 31st. Because our end-of-the-year fundraising runs over a period of several months, it makes sense to break the effort down into smaller chunks. For instance, we might start to brainstorm ideas about our EOY fundraising effort in August, do the goal setting in September, plan the marketing tactics in October, launch the effort in November, and push hard to a conclusion in December.

When planning the year-end effort, remember what else is already going on in the organization. Don't overload team members.

Solicit input from others to make sure the deadlines are realistic and achievable.

 Make allowances for the unforeseen. The unexpected will always rear its ugly head at the most inopportune times.

Write Down the Goals

A plan worth doing merits recording. The written plan can be simple or exhaustive—you decide. A simple fundraising plan might include the task to be done, the resources needed, along with who will do what when. It may not need to be more complex than that.

You might decide to use an online project management program to track the deadlines or a WORD document or EXCEL spreadsheet to assign tasks.

 **Don't tie yourself to a system that manages you instead of you being in charge. There are more than a few project management systems that demand loads of time before they spit out the needed information.**

Develop an Action to Achieve the Goals

Author's Note: It made more sense at this writing to give the planning stage, which is normally part of the goal setting process, its own chapter instead of including it here. You'll find the action plan talked about in Chapter SIX – Setting Things in Motion.

Stay Focused—Don't Get Sidetracked

Goal setting is an ongoing process. As the fundraising process proceeds things may need adjusting. The original estimates may be too high or too low.

Perhaps the email campaigns are working better than the Facebook ads. If that's the case, turn off what's not working and boost what is showing positive results.

Resist what's known in the industry as scope creep. That's where people take their eye off the ball and start going in different directions or expand the original goals too far.

Ignite Your Fundraising

6 Goal Setting Takeaways:

1. Set goals that motivate the team.
2. Make sure the goals are in line with the organization's mission.
3. Use the SMART method when setting your goals.
4. Record the goals (on paper or in the cloud).
5. Develop an action plan to achieve the goals.
6. Stay focused—don't get sidetracked.

Try to handle one pressing issue at a time, do it well—Everything with Excellence, then move on.

 Constantly recast the vision and keep the group excited about the prospect of reaching the goals that were set.

 **Find a Goal Setting Example, Project Priority and Goal Setting Worksheets at the end of this chapter.**

Project Priority Example

> Project Priority Example
>
> *"Everything with Excellence"*
>
> **Project One:** Finish manuscript for *Ignite Your Fundraising*. Proof copy and downloadable examples and worksheets.
>
> Urgency: April 1, 2018   Cost: _____   Priority: 1
>
> **Project Two:** Draft email series to announce Ignite Your Fundraising online webinar on April 15, 2018. Start sending out emails April 1, 2018.
>
> Urgency: April 15, 2018   Cost: _____   Priority: 2
>
> **Project Three:** Create webinar slide deck for presentation on April 15, 2018
>
> Urgency: April 15, 2018   Cost: _____   Priority: 3
>
> **Project Four:** Create social media announcements for April webinar.
>
> Urgency: April 5, 2018   Cost: _____   Priority: 4
>
> **Project Five:** Hold Ignite Your Fundraising webinar on April 15, 2018. Release *Ignite Your Fundraising* book.
>
> Urgency: April 15, 2018   Cost: _____   Priority: 5
>
> Copyright © 2018 ministryTHRIVE

Download at:

ministrythrive.com/ProjectPriorityExample.pdf

Ignite Your Fundraising

Project Priority Worksheet

Project Priority Worksheet

"Everything with Excellence"

Project One: _____
_____

Urgency: _____ Cost: _____ Priority: _____

Project Two: _____
_____

Urgency: _____ Cost: _____ Priority: _____

Project Three: _____
_____

Urgency: _____ Cost: _____ Priority: _____

Project Four: _____
_____

Urgency: _____ Cost: _____ Priority: _____

Project Five: _____
_____

Urgency: _____ Cost: _____ Priority: _____

Copyright © 2018 ministryTHRIVE

Download at:

ministrythrive.com/ProjectPriorityWorksheet.docx

SMART Goal Setting Example

SMART Goal Setting Example
"Everything with Excellence"

Project One:
Launch the Ignition Learning Series. These educational materials (mostly books) will be directed at two non-profit audiences. First, those organizations that are either in start-up mode, who have stalled out somewhere along the way, or have not yet been able to raise $10,000 or more per year. The secondary audience is those organizations that have raised between $50,000 and $100,000 but desire their fundraising efforts to be more effective and efficient.

Specific:
The first book in this series will focus on year-end fundraising. It's title: *Ignite Your Fundraising*. Develop and hold workshops based on the learnings. Collect feedback to ensure the materials are most useful. Develop a slide deck and present a Go-to-Meeting webinar to introduce the educational materials to projects worldwide. It is important the webinar be available on-demand. Use Createspace (Amazon.com) to publish and sell the books. Include examples, worksheets, info card and other documents to give projects a jumpstart on creating their own fundraising materials.

Measurable:
The webinar – 80 attendees on April 15, 2018
The book – sell 300 copies by June 30, 2018, sell 1,000 copies by September 31, 2018
The webinar – 400 downloads by September 1, 2018, 1,000 downloads by December 31, 2018

Attainable:
200 projects have been identified in the state of Colorado. Hopefully 80 will attend the April 15, 2018 webinar.

Relevant:
Book chapters: Deciding on Your Fundraising Goals, Acquiring New Donors, Telling a Great Story, Getting Your Message Out, Setting Things in Motion, Following Up, Measuring Your Success, Getting Better Results and End-of-the-year Fundraising.

Time Bound:
Finish book manuscript by April 1, 2018, finish webinar slide deck by April 10, 2018, ready book for publishing and sale by April 1, 2018, hold webinar on April 15, 2018 and announce book for sale on April 15, 2018.

Copyright © 2018 ministryTHRIVE

Download at:

ministrythrive.com/SMARTGoalSettingExample.pdf

Ignite Your Fundraising

SMART Goal Setting Worksheet

SMART Goal Setting Worksheet

"Everything with Excellence"

Project One: _____

Specific: _____
_____

Measurable: _____
_____

Attainable: _____
_____

Relevant: _____
_____

Time Bound: _____
_____

Copyright © 2018 ministryTHRIVE

Download at:

ministrythrive.com/SMARTGoalSettingWorksheet.docx

Acquiring New Donors

"It always seems impossible until it's done." — Nelson Mandela

The fundraising process is also the perfect time to work on acquiring new donors. If you're new to the fundraising game or if you've stalled out somewhere along in the process of collecting your first 100 potential donors to contact, then this chapter is for you. This section also deals with acquiring new donors past the "100" mark.

Let's talk about those trying to attain their first 100 names then we'll move on to those organizations that would like to increase the number of names in their donor file.

"I don't know 100 people."

Over the life of the organization your potential donors are going to come from three people groups: family and friends (the smallest), people who know people you may not (much larger), and the people who are complete strangers to you (the largest).

It's natural to start with the first group, "family and friends." But if you don't get past this segment your fundraising efforts will eventually stall and the organization's existence may be in peril.

What percentage of donors do you know personally? If that number is anywhere near 100%, your organization's reach past family and friends is almost nonexistent. You must expand your reach past this first people group if the organization is going to thrive and survive into the future.

Now, you may not be able to come up with your first 100 names in one sitting, but it will be possible over time. It will certainly take an amount of thought and of reflection on your part.

Don't eliminate people's names as you build your list of potential contacts. Let them make the choice not to be involved. You could eliminate an ardent supporter or major donor, not knowing their passion.

Here's a list of contact group possibilities to get you thinking about your first 100 names:

- Family and friends

Ignite Your Fundraising

- Your acquaintances at church (past churches?)
- Those from small groups you've attended
- Neighbors (past neighbors?)
- Those you work with (past business associates?)
- Friends from college
- Friends from social, civic, or professional organizations
- Professionals that cross your path (doctors, lawyers, accountants, teachers)
- Contractors (plumbers, heating & air conditioning specialists, landscapers, handymen)

You'll need to work on your list over several days or perhaps a few weeks. Keep coming back to the list as names come to mind.

 **Find a First 100 Names Worksheet at the end of this chapter.**

As you build your list, decide what information you'd like to gather about each prospective donor. At first, perhaps their name, email address, and phone number may be sufficient.

Later you'll want to start to classify people based on how they respond, their interests in the projects you have going, plus how and when they donate.

Don't ask people for more personal information than you initially plan to use. It's only natural for the individual to think they'll receive something in the mail if they give up their street address.

70% of Americans give to charitable organizations. People that give, give and people who don't, don't. The number one indicator of a person giving to your organization is that they're already giving elsewhere.

Don't wait to start setting appointments until you have exactly 100 names on your list—that practice may be akin to procrastination. The sooner you get started on setting appointments the more at ease you'll be with the process going forward and the sooner you'll be on your way to raising the funds needed by your organization.

How to Reach People

Acquiring new donors is a three-step process. First, you'll have to set an appointment to meet with the person. Second, during that initial meeting you'll want to share what God's doing and your story—the passion of why you do what you do. This is not the time to ask them to donate—that comes later.

The goal of the first meeting is really to set a second time to talk.

Once the person understands the organization's mission and you've shared your passion then you'll want them to go home, talk with their spouse, consider being involved in whatever way, and to ask God how they should proceed.

Think about walking onto a car lot. You don't point to the first car you see and tell the salesperson, "I'll take that one." You ask questions, kick the tires, open the hood, take it for a test-drive, and perhaps even go home and think long and hard about the purchase, and the financing. People donating to a cause are not much different.

The question uppermost in every potential donor's mind when you first meet will be, "**Why should I give to this organization instead of another worthwhile cause?**"

Focus on **why** you're doing what you do not the **what**, **how,** and **when**. Yes, it's good to tell people you're involved in building a medical clinic in a small out of the way village in the Congo. Yes, it's important to tell the potential donors the care it will provide the locals once opened. And it's even relevant to tell them when the work will be completed.

But, it's most important for people to know "**why**" you're doing what you're doing. The clinic will improve people's lives. There will be less disease. Healthier birth rates. Longer lifespans. Less suffering. A better quality of life all around.

Once they understand your mission and hear your passion they can make the best decision on how/if they should be involved.

Give people various ways to be involved. Perhaps they can join the advisory team, volunteer, or share their talents or gifts at some point. Fundraising is not always about the money.

Let's breakdown the appointment process further.

Setting an Appointment

You'll need a script to keep you on track and to make sure you say everything that needs saying when you place the appointment phone calls.

Your script does not have to be a word-for-word speech—it's a quick reference guide in case you get lost or to keep you from forgetting what to say.

 **Find an Appointment Setting Script Example and Worksheet at the end of this chapter.**

Remember, the goal of this first call is to gain an occasion to meet with the person.

Here are 6 Appointment Setting Takeaways to keep in mind:

Ignite Your Fundraising

6 Appointment Setting Takeaways:

1. Establish clear goals.
2. Ask if they have a few minutes to chat.
3. Stick to the script.
4. Offer a choice of days and times to meet.
5. Confirm the appointment details when ending the call.
6. Don't forget to listen.

Have a backup plan if people do not have time to talk or if they say "no" to meeting.

If they say it's not a convenient time to talk, ask if you can call at another time. Be specific…Tuesday evening better…next week Wednesday?

If they say it's not a good time to meet, ask if you can send them information about the organization and then perhaps follow up to answer any questions.

Focus on telling people where your heart is. This is an opportunity to work where God is doing great things. It's not always about giving money to the cause.

 **Find Information and Donor Card examples at the end of this chapter.**

Ignite Your Fundraising

So, let's say you land your first appointment. Now what?

Your First Face-to-face Meeting

Get organized before meeting. Make sure you have the items you'd like to share: business card, brochure, video, whatever.

You'll need a second script when you do meet with people. It serves the same purpose as the one used for setting your appointments—it keeps you on track and makes sure what needs to be covered is talked about.

 **Find a Face-to-face Meeting Script Example and Worksheet at the end of this chapter.**

Do a run-through of the conversation script in hand. If a trusted colleague can listen to your presentation all the better. The more often you practice your delivery the more comfortable and confident you'll become.

Here are five reasons why Craig Jarrow, the Time Management Ninja, believes face-to-face meetings—Get it done:

1. Body language plays a major role in how we communicate with people
2. Ensures engagement
3. Helps clarify things—it's hard to raise your hand while on the phone

4. Drives participation
5. Tends to be more efficient

You'll obviously be able to see the other person's reaction as well as measure their interest level in what you say during your time together.

Here are 6 Face-to-face Meeting Takeaways to keep in mind:

6 Face-to-face Meeting Takeaways:

1. Talk about your spiritual journey, how you got to where you are today.
2. Talk about the ministry's purpose (what's the problem, what's the solution, why you, and why now?)
3. Ask if they would be willing to consider ways they might be involved—mention how others are helping the cause.
4. Close with a final thought.
5. Ask if you can check back with them in 7 to 10 days—ask if they prefer an email or phone call.
6. Thank them for listening.

Mahdi Roghanizad, a Huron University College Department of Management and Organizational Studies professor, said, *"that despite the speed of email, making a request to a person face-to-face is considerably more effective—34 times more effective."*

People Who Know People You May Not Know

The second group of potential prospects and donors will come from people your family and friends know that you may not be acquainted with.

It works best if family members or friends provide you with an introduction before you call the person or set an appointment.

How about asking your family or friends to invite a few couples over to their homes? These types of gatherings provide a comfortable place to have coffee and dessert while everyone gets to know you. You could give a 20-minute presentation and then pass out information on the organization along with a card to collect their personal information. Next step? Follow up and schedule an appointment.

There are those that may not agree, but this would not be the best time to ask for a gift. The purpose of these social events is to inform people of what God's doing and what you believe your calling is.

 This is a time to build relationships. People need to get to know you.

The real goal of this first meeting is to schedule a second time where they can better understand your work and you can learn more about the others in attendance. You need to understand what they're passion about. If their passion connects with yours it's more likely they'll support your cause.

Ignite Your Fundraising

Of course, there may be people that want to give on the spot. Be prepared to make the donation process simple and straightforward. Always leave information behind so people can think about giving. Refer them to your website or Facebook page for more information.

Always ask people if you can send them your newsletter or email updates. Don't assume people want to hear from you unless the box on your information card w=is checked. It's important to have a box people can check. Why send information to people that may not want to hear from you?

Don't make the ask too early. People need to be informed before they make their decision to become involved.

Speak at Gatherings

Another method of meeting people whom you may not know would be to speak to a Sunday School Class, Bible Study, or Small Group.

Again, the goal here is to collect contact information so you can call for appointments later.

Relationships come before gifts. Don't put the cart before the horse.

People Who Are Complete Strangers

Reaching out to people who have never heard about your organization will be more challenging.

Reaching out to strangers will strain the budget but are necessary if the organization is to survive and grow.

Here are ideas from other organizations that find themselves in the same place. You'll have to decide which ideas seem to be the best fit for your organization.

- Approach your most faithful donors and ask them if they would be willing to contact their colleagues. Perhaps they would be willing to host small, informal gatherings. This is known as peer-to-peer fundraising.
- Leverage your board or advisory team members to see if they would be interested in hosting similar gatherings.
- Try retargeting your prospective donor/donor groups to make sure you have not overlooked anyone.
- Investigate online crowdfunding to see if your organization is a good fit for this strategy.
- There are organizations who purchase lists of people currently giving to other organizations. Remember, givers give.
- Social media may be a good avenue to prospect for new donors. Start conversations on social platforms that agree with your values. You may be able to attract people from those

platforms to your website or social presence whether it be Facebook, Instagram, *et al.*

- You may also want to enter the fray of Facebook advertising. It can be quite effective when used strategically for the right cause.

You also need to find ways to raise the visibility of your organization. Here are thoughts in that direction:

- Speak at local and national events.
- Write guest posts for other blog sites.
- Find ways to be visible if your organization is locally-based by volunteering or being involved.
- Write for publications your prospective donors and supporters are likely to read.
- Have your local TV outlet do a story on the organization.
- Have your local newspaper do a feature.
- Form alliances with similar groups or organizations that do not directly compete in your space.
- Contact local radio stations to gain an interview.
- Network. Network. Network.
- Post "hero" photos of the work your organization is doing on sites like Instagram and Pinterest.

 **Have a brainstorming session with your board or team to come up with ideas you believe are congruent with your organization's mission.**

Ignite Your Fundraising

First 100 Names Worksheet

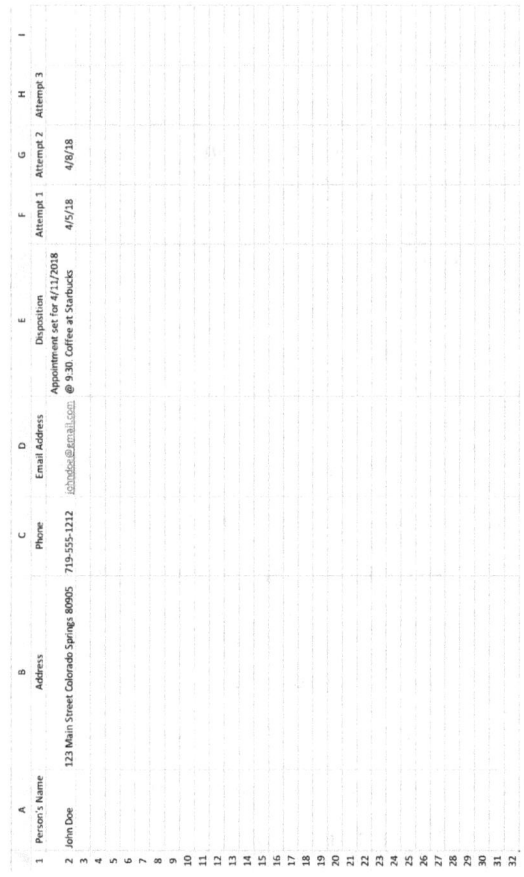

Download at:

ministrythrive.com/First100NamesWorksheet.xlsx

Appointment Setting Script Example

Appointment Setting Script Example

Greeting:

Hey Bill...John Calling.

Spend a few minutes finding out what's happening in Bills' life.
Show interest, don't just change the subject.
Be willing to listen if Bill has something to share.

Why You're Calling:

Make sure it's a good time to talk.
If not, ask when you can call back.
Let the person know upfront you're not calling to ask for a gift.
Briefly let them know what God's been up to and how it's affecting you.
Describe what you're working on.

The goal of this call is to set an appointment to meet NOT to receive a gift.

Set an Appointment:

Ask if you can meet with them for a cup of coffee or lunch if they have time.

Tell them the appointment time will last no longer than 30 minutes.
Expand on what God's been up to and how it's affecting you.
Give more details about how you're involved.

If the answer is no:
If they don't have time to meet or would rather not meet...ask if they would be willing to receive periodic emails from you and if they would be willing to pray about what you're involved in. (Don't just start sending them information unless they say yes.)

Confirm the Appointment Details:

Confirm what's been agreed upon. The location, date and time.

Thank them for their willingness to meet.

Show excitement at the prospect of meeting.

Copyright © 2018 ministryTHRIVE

Download at:

ministrythrive.com/AppointmentSettingScriptExample.pdf

Chapter 2/Acquiring New Donors

Ignite Your Fundraising

Appointment Setting Script Worksheet

Appointment Setting Script Worksheet

Greeting: _____

Why you're calling: _____

Set an Appointment: _____

If the answer is no: _____

Close: (details, clear, directions, date, time) _____

Copyright © 2018 ministryTHR!VE

Download at:

ministrythrive.com/AppointmentSettingScriptWorksheet.docx

Ignite Your Fundraising

Information Card Example

[Information card with fields: Name, Phone, Email, What interests the person most?, Add you to our mailing list? Yes ___ No ___ Next Contact Date: ___]

[Second card with Comments field]

Download at:

ministrythrive.com/InformationCardExample.docx

Ignite Your Fundraising

Donor Card Example

Download at:

ministrythrive.com/DonorCardExample.docx

Ignite Your Fundraising

Face-to-face Meeting Script Example

Face-to-face Meeting Script Example

Name: John Doe
Phone: 719-555-1212
Email: john@website.com
Relationship: Friend of Bill P.

Meeting Date/Time: 3/28 @ 9:00 Place: Starbucks on Centennial Blvd.

Start with some small talk in order to get to know more about the individual—their family, their interests, other ministries they might be supporting. Take good notes.

Talk about your spiritual journey, how you got to where you are today:

Hearing God's Call...

After leaving Egypt and a series of events, including the parting of the Red Sea, and being led by a pillar of fire, the Israelites found themselves on the banks of the Jordan River, opposite the Promised Land. God said the land flowed with milk and honey. Moses dispatches twelve trusted spies that included Aaron and Caleb to survey the land. Upon their return, the intelligence reports were good and bad. Yes, the land flowed with milk and honey. God was right. But, the people of the land were strong, the cities were large and well-fortified, and moreover, the descendants of Anak, giants, lived there.

The hearts of the Israelites fell. As they started to murmur and complain to Moses, Caleb stepped forwarded, quieted the crowd and proclaimed: "Let's go up and take the land—now. We can do it." Numbers 13:30 (MSG)

Project:Caleb exists to assist groups and organizations in devising a plan, gathering the intelligence, weighing the findings, developing an action plan and "taking the land" which God has called one to conquer.

Talk about the ministries purpose and what you're trying to accomplish: What's the need, What's the solution, Why you, and Why now?

What's the need?

Those involved in ministry want to spend as much time with these activities as possible and rightfully so. These same people are however not that experienced with the planning, marketing and fundraising chores that go hand-and-hand with ministry. To help these project managers succeed, it makes sense for Project:Caleb to shore up these gaps in experience, by offering coaching and educational services.

What's the solution?

Project:Caleb offers its services in a variety of ways for several reasons. First, those heading up the projects come from varied backgrounds and have different experience levels and skills. These same project managers are also dispersed across the country and around the world. To be as practical as possible, Project:Caleb offers its services in-person, over the phone or by Internet facilities such as SKYPE and Go-To-Meeting.

Copyright © 2018 ministryTHRIVE

Download at:

ministrythrive.com/Face-to-faceMeetingScriptExample.pdf

Ignite Your Fundraising

Face-to-face Meeting Script Example

> **Why you?**
>
> Project:Caleb has more than 30 years of experience building businesses along with more than 50 years in technology. John has authored 13 books and taught hundreds of workshops and seminars. He has designed and developed training programs used worldwide. He also has more than 30 years of experience launching and working with non-profits and ministries as well as 15 years of board experience – mostly as chairman of the board and president of past organizations.
>
> **Why now?**
>
> There is no better time to preach Jesus than now. The projects in New Horizons and Joy to the World Foundations are working hard to accomplish God's leading in a variety of ways from healthcare to education and spiritual development to dignity of life issues and desperately need assistance in the areas of planning, marketing, fundraising and donor development. Project:Caleb is well-prepared to aid in these areas.
>
> **Ask if they would be willing to consider ways they might be involved—mention how others are helping.**
>
> **Close with a final thought.**
>
> **Ask if you can check back with them in 5 to 7 days—ask if they prefer being contacted by email or phone.**
>
> *Need to check back on April 2, 2018 by email.*
>
> **Thank them for listening.**
>
> Copyright © 2018 ministryTHRIVE

Download at:

ministrythrive.com/Face-to-faceMeetingScriptExample.pdf

Ignite Your Fundraising

Face-to-face Meeting Script Example

> **Meeting Comments:**
> John Doe was very receptive. He's interested in hearing more after he has some time to consider how he might be involved. Need to send second brochure for him to give to a friend.
>
> Copyright © 2018 ministryTHRIVE

Download at:
ministrythrive.com/Face-to-faceMeetingScriptExample.pdf

Ignite Your Fundraising

Face-to-face Meeting Script Worksheet

Face-to-face Meeting Script Worksheet

Name: _____

Phone: _____

Email: _____

Relationship: _____

Meeting Date/Time: _____ Place: _____

Start with some small talk in order to get to know more about the individual—their family, their interests, other ministries they might be supporting. Take good notes.

_____
_____
_____

Talk about your spiritual journey, how you got to where you are today:

_____
_____
_____

Talk about the ministries purpose and what you're trying to accomplish: What's the need, What's the solution, Why you, and Why now?

What's the need:
_____
_____

What's the solution:
_____
_____

Why you? _____
_____

Copyright © 2018 ministryTHRIVE

Download at:

ministrythrive.com/Face-to-faceMeetingScriptWorksheet.docx

Ignite Your Fundraising

Face-to-face Meeting Script Worksheet

Why now? _____

Ask if they would be willing to consider ways they might be involved—mention how others are helping.

Close with a final thought.

Ask if you can check back with them in 5 to 7 days—ask if they prefer being contacted by email or phone.

Thank them for listening.

Meeting Comments:
_____
_____
_____
_____
_____
_____
_____
_____

Copyright © 2018 ministryTHRIVE

Download at:

ministrythrive.com/Face-to-faceMeetingScriptWorksheet.docx

Telling a Great Story

"I like a good story well told. That is the reason I am sometimes forced to tell them myself." —
Mark Twain

There's no substitute for telling a compelling story that gets positive results. Everyone loves hearing or reading a great story.

An organization can spend their entire fundraising budget on Facebook ads or sending out weekly email salvos, and without a great story attached, the fundraising outcome will likely be disappointing.

Telling a great story draws the reader in, tells how the problem is being solved, and leaves no doubt in the reader's mind on how the money, once donated, is making an enormous impact.

Write, then edit. It's near impossible to constantly stop the creative process and shift gears to the diagnostic phase.

Here's a list of thoughts that come to mind when thinking about constructing a great story:

- Every great story has a purpose.
- Has a hook.
- Draws the reader into the story as soon as possible.
- Don't wander.
- Keeps it real by using "hero" photos and exact details.
- Brief storytelling works best.
- Taps into the reader's emotions.
- Does the reader see their self in this situation?
- Brings in those being affected.

 Find a Tell a Great Story Worksheet at the end of this chapter.

Let's examine the elements that make up a great story:

Every Great Story Has a Purpose

Whether in an email, newsletter, Facebook ad, or blog post, the question, "Why are you writing this story in the first place?" crosses the reader's mind. There needs to be a goal, a reason, an intent. Why are you expending your time and energy while asking the reader to invest theirs? The goal might be to educate potential donors. It may be to encourage people to get involved in the work at a deeper level. You might be making a plea at the end of the year.

 Decide on the goals before the writing begins.

Have a Hook

Every great story has a hook, usually the first sentence as the book is opened. The "hook" grabs the reader's attention and piques their curiosity. They end up wanting to know more. Harper Lee starts *To Kill a Mocking Bird* out by writing, "When he was nearly thirteen, my brother Jem got his arm badly broken at the elbow." Wow, what happened? J. R. R. Tolkien starts The Hobbit this way, "In a hole in the ground there lived a hobbit. Not a dirty, nasty, wet hole, filled with the ends of worms, and an oozy smell, nor yet a dry, bare, sandy hole with nothing in it to sit down on or to eat: it was a hobbit-hole, and that means comfort."

Craft a compelling first sentence (or headline) and you're well on your way to grabbing the reader's attention and telling a great story.

Draw the Reader into the Story as Soon as Possible

Draw the reader into the story by not using words such as: we, us and ours. Those words tend to remove the reader from the story. Use language the reader is familiar with seeing. Don't get bogged down in too many details too soon. Start to develop a storyline. Let the reader know where you're taking him or her. The reader is investing time. They need to know you won't be wasting it.

 Surveys state the average human attention span is approximately 8 seconds.

Don't Wander

Avoid introducing too many facets of what's happening on the ground even though they all may be exciting. The reader may become confused. If you have several accounts to tell then write several short, separate stories. Stay at a level of detail the reader is familiar with and avoid getting too far into the weeds.

 Get over your perfectionist tendencies. Write.

Keep It Real by Using Photos and Exact Details

Photos of the location or action shots create interest. Posed photos of children standing outside their orphanage do little to bring excitement to the story. Children playing, standing in line to receive their shots, or receiving gift packages end up showcasing the project's impact. Few things warm a person's heart more than seeing children smiling, playing or having fun. These are known as "hero" photos.

Make sure to tell people what's happening in the photos; don't assume.

Brief Storytelling Works Best

There's no reason to compile a novelette when a short story will do. People's time is precious and competition for their attention is fierce.

There are accepted writing standards out there and they should be followed. A newsletter can be longer than a blog post. A post on Facebook can be longer than the text associated with a picture sent on Instagram. Stick with what everyone is expecting. Emails that droll on are hardly ever started or finished for that matter. Long emails usually find their way into the recipient's trash folder before being read.

Tap into the Reader's Emotions

It's important to share your passion for what God is doing along with tapping into the reader's emotions. Don't keep things dry and detached. How is the work that is being done affecting the lives of the people on the ground? Talk about the victories as well as the challenges. Talk about lives being changed. Share your feelings and the feelings of the beneficiaries.

Can the Reader See Their Self in this Situation?

Try and find ways for the reader to see himself or herself in the story. Can they see themselves doing the work? Can they see themselves as happy as you are when describing the events? Remember, there may be a great distance between the reader and what's happening overseas. That gap needs to be closed as much as possible.

Bring in Those Being Affected

There is no real substitute for hearing from the families or children, being touched in positive ways by the organization's efforts. A quote or two within the story lends incredible veracity to the tale being told.

 Use "hero" photos whenever possible.

Here are 6 Story Telling Takeaways to keep in mind:

<u>6 Story Telling Takeaways:</u>

1. Every great story has a purpose.
2. Have a hook.
3. Draw the reader into the story as soon as possible.
4. Don't wander.
5. Keep it real by using "hero" photos and details.
6. Be the writing as brief as possible.

Good luck telling your next *great* story.

Ignite Your Fundraising

Telling a Great Story Worksheet

> Telling a Great Story
> Worksheet
>
> Okay, now that we have a good idea of what goes into telling a great story, let's answer the seven questions that opened this chapter. First, jot down your ideas on these Show & Tell pages. Then open a document and start writing.
>
> Here's a writing tip: Don't write and edit at the same time. First let the ideas flow, and then come back and put your editor's hat on to polish the copy.
>
> **What's our purpose in writing?**
>
> _____
> _____
> _____
>
> **How do we make the story compelling?**
>
> _____
> _____
> _____
>
> **How can we share our passion?**
>
> _____
> _____
> _____
> _____
>
> **How do we keep it real with photos and stories?**
>
> _____
> _____
> _____
>
> Copyright © 2018 ministryTHRIVE

Download at:

ministrythrive.com/TellingAGreatStoryWorksheet.docx

Ignite Your Fundraising

Telling a Great Story Worksheet

> How do we tap into the donor's (reader's) emotions?
>
> How can the donor see themselves in the story?
>
> Copyright © 2018 ministryTHRIVE

Download at:

ministrythrive.com/TellingAGreatStoryWorksheet.docx

Chapter 3/Telling a Great Story

FOUR

Getting Your Message Out

"Marketing is no longer about the stuff that you make, but about the stories you tell." —
Seth Godin

Not all donors are created equal. Donors have different wants and needs. Some donors will give once, others monthly, some as needs of an organization are made known.

 **Most studies show that people give 12 months a year when using direct deposit. Relying on people to remember is send in their gift on a regular basis has some pitfalls. For example, people may forget, or they may be faced with a family emergency.**

Certain donors can give more than others. There are donors who have abilities or experience the organization can use more than money.

Ignite Your Fundraising

Donors have different interests. You may have a group of people who are interested in infrastructure projects such as drilling a well, building a medical clinic, or raising a new dormitory for the girls. There are donors who may be interested in the agriculture needs of remote villages.

 Match the message to the donor's interest.

 Even though all donors are not the same, they all need to be treated with respect and gratitude.

You'll need to understand what your donors are passionate about.

Donors Differ

Once you have that information in hand, you'll be able to communicate with them on their terms about the various organizational needs.

 **Here's a communication method to keep in mind—younger donors will be more accessible on their smartphones and will likely gravitate more to quick, brief messages and videos than older generations.**

There are donors who will prefer the newsletter be mailed while others may be more comfortable reading blogs online.

Certain donors will gravitate to social media while others, for example, have no intention of ever creating a Facebook, Snapchat, or Instagram account.

What we're saying here is fundraisers need to have a three-prong approach:

- Understand each donor's passion and interest.
- Be aware of their communication preferences.
- Appreciate the fact that donors do not give equally.

You'll want to design a Communication Plan that incorporates these elements.

Your Communication Plan

The Communication Plan is what takes place when you want to get your message out to supporters and prospective donors. In *Chapter SIX – Following Up* we'll talk about how to thank donors for the contributions and follow up with them until the fundraising campaign ends.

 Keep the focus on the donor not the organization.

Reporting on the organization's progress and impact promptly, or at all, seem to be missing from many organizations. Donors want, need to know their money is being spent wisely on the projects they are most passionate about.

As we've said before, a communication plan is really nothing more than deciding what to say, to whom, when, and by what means. Of course, there's a goal component in that we want the communication that takes place between the organization and individuals to generate an action—preferably in the form of acquiring a new email address or receiving a gift.

Let's look at the "what to say", to whom", "when", and "by what means" components:

What to Say?

First, highlight the stories you believe people would be most interested in hearing, then sprinkle in other information. Who knows, something they read may spark their interest in a different direction.

Remember, we're supposed to be thinking of ways we can incorporate the eleven bulleted items that were listed at the beginning of this chapter.

 Always talk about how the funds are being spent and the impact the money is making.

Use details, personal stories, and loads of "hero" photos. Be specific.

To Whom?

Prospective **donors** and supporters have very different interests; and may not all be up to speed on the same details.

Potential **donors** typically need to be educated—they need to be brought up to speed on what's been happening as well as how they can be involved today.

Donors who are on board, have already shown that they are interested in what's happening. They need to know their money is being spent wisely. They need to be constantly reassured the projects are making good progress and people's lives are being changed.

When?

Major, or anchor, donors should be contacted on a regular basis perhaps by phone if possible. They'll want more details and depth than the one-time donor.

Those that support the organization's efforts monthly should be contacted at the same interval—monthly.

Donors should be sent more information beyond what prospective **donors** receive. Perhaps brief hand-written notes would due.

By What Means?

Prospective donors and supporters need to be informed or contacted regarding their preferences.

For example, specific people may prefer to be contacted by phone or SKYPE. Of course, this works while the organization's donor file is small. Contacting donors in person becomes near impossible as the organization becomes sizeable.

Some donors may want to be informed by US Mail. Each organization will have to make the call as to the profitability of using street mail.

 Think about adding a line to your donor card highlighting the amount, the impact and the timeframe related to the fundraising campaign.

With the advent of the Internet, there are a variety of channels, many free of charge, that can be used to communicate with prospective donors and supporters. Each organization will have to decide which platforms work best for the skills of their team and the donor's preferences.

Here are 6 Getting Your Message Out Takeaways to keep in mind:

6 Getting Your Message Out Takeaways:

1. Resist treating every donor the same.

2. Know your donor's passion.
3. Understand your donor's communication preferences.
4. Make the conversations two-way.
5. Report on progress and impact.
6. Be consistent—it builds expectation.

 **Find a Sample Communication Plan by Donor Schedule at the end of this chapter.**

Ignite Your Fundraising

Sample Communication Plan By Donor Schedule

Sample Communication Plan
By Donor Schedule

Here's what a yearly schedule might look like when communicating with all three donor types. Let's say the three groups all start giving in January.

January
One-time Gift
   Immediate
   Tax deductible receipt sent by email.
   Within 24 Hours
   Personalized email thanking the person and highlight the gift's impact.
Monthly Gift
   Immediate
   Tax deductible receipt sent by email.
   Within 24 Hours
   Phone call is possible thanking the person and highlight the gift's impact.
Major Donor
   Immediate
   Tax deductible receipt sent by email.
   Within 24 Hours
   Phone call thanking the person and highlight the gift's impact

February
One-time Gift   Personalized email highlighting their gift and the project's impact.
Monthly Gift   Personalized email highlighting their gift and the project's impact.
Major Gift   Phone calls highlighting their gift and the project's impact. Follow up by email with details of the phone call.
   Phone call telling another donor's story on how supporting the project is changing their life. Followed up by email with details of the phone call.

March
One-time Gift   Personalized email telling another donor's story on how supporting the project is changing their life. Ask for a second gift.
Monthly Gift   Personalized email telling another donor's story on how supporting the project is changing their life.
Major Gift   Phone calls highlighting their gift and the project's impact. Follow up by email with details of the phone call.
Major Gift   Phone call telling another donor's story on how supporting the project is changing their life. Followed up by email with details of the phone call.

April
Monthly Gift   Personalized email highlighting their gift and the project's impact.
Monthly Gift   Email newsletter recap of past successes and needs.

Copyright © 2018 ministryTHRIVE

Download at:

ministrythrive.com/SampleCommunicationPlanDonorSchedule.pdf

Ignite Your Fundraising

Sample Communication Plan By Donor Schedule

	Sample Communication Plan By Donor Schedule
Major Gift	Phone calls highlighting their gift and the project's impact. Follow up by email with details of the phone call.
	Phone call telling another donor's story on how supporting the project is changing their life. Followed up by email with details of the phone call.
Major Gift	Email newsletter recap of past successes and needs.
May	
Monthly Gift	Personalized email telling another donor's story on how supporting the project is changing their life.
Major Gift	Phone calls highlighting their gift and the project's impact. Follow up by email with details of the phone call.
	Phone call telling another donor's story on how supporting the project is changing their life. Followed up by email with details of the phone call.
June	
Monthly Gift	Personalized email highlighting their gift and the project's impact.
Major Gift	Phone calls highlighting their gift and the project's impact. Follow up by email with details of the phone call.
	Phone call telling another donor's story on how supporting the project is changing their life. Followed up by email with details of the phone call.
July	
One-time Gift	Personalized email highlighting project's impact.
	Email newsletter recap of past successes and needs.
Monthly Gift	Personalized email telling another donor's story on how supporting the project is changing their life.
Monthly Gift	Email newsletter recap of past successes and needs.
Major Gift	Phone calls highlighting their gift and the project's impact. Follow up by email with details of the phone call.
	Phone call telling another donor's story on how supporting the project is changing their life. Followed up by email with details of the phone call.
Major Gift	Email newsletter recap of past successes and needs.
August	
Monthly Gift	Personalized email highlighting their gift and the project's impact.
Major Gift	Phone calls highlighting their gift and the project's impact. Follow up by email with details of the phone call.
	Phone call telling another donor's story on how supporting the project is changing their life. Followed up by email with details of the phone call.

Copyright © 2018 ministryTHRIVE

Download at:

ministrythrive.com/SampleCommunicationPlanDonorSchedule.pdf

Ignite Your Fundraising

Sample Communication Plan
By Donor Schedule

Sample Communication Plan
By Donor Schedule

September
Monthly Gift — Personalized email telling another donor's story on how supporting the project is changing their life.
Major Gift — Phone calls highlighting their gift and the project's impact. Follow up by email with details of the phone call.

Phone call telling another donor's story on how supporting the project is changing their life. Followed up by email with details of the phone call.

October
One-time Gift — Personalized email highlighting project's impact.
Email newsletter recap of past successes and needs.
Monthly Gift — Personalized email highlighting their gift and the project's impact.
Monthly Gift — Email newsletter recap of past successes and needs.
Major Gift — Phone calls highlighting their gift and the project's impact. Follow up by email with details of the phone call.

Phone call telling another donor's story on how supporting the project is changing their life. Followed up by email with details of the phone call.

Major Gift — Email newsletter recap of past successes and needs.
November
One-time Gift — See Sample EOY Communication Plan Schedule.
Monthly Gift — See Sample EOY Communication Plan Schedule.
Major Gift — See Sample EOY Communication Plan Schedule.
December
One-time Gift — See Sample EOY Communication Plan Schedule.
Monthly Gift — See Sample EOY Communication Plan Schedule.
Major Gift — See Sample EOY Communication Plan Schedule.

Copyright © 2018 ministryTHRIVE

Download at:

ministrythrive.com/SampleCommunicationPlanDonorSchedule.pdf

Setting Things In Motion

"Can I be excused for the rest of my life?" —
SpongeBob SquarePants

Planning the execution of a project is not everyone's strong suit. There are roughly 99 doers for every one planner out there. Most people want to jump into a project and begin to get things done. It's a laudable goal, but possibly not always the best approach.

Thinking needs to take place first.

Think about going on vacation. You'll need to pick a destination, gas up the car, grab a map or GPS device, pack the trunk, and corral the kids in the car before taking off.

Staring at a blank sheet of paper trying to decide how to plan the execution of the project can be daunting.

Fundraising campaigns have a number of moving parts: there are the tasks to be accomplished, when they'll happen, who will be responsible, what resources and skills will be needed, along with a set of deadlines.

Here we use a sample end-of-the-year fundraising plan that runs from August through January.

Developing an Action Plan

You may be an individual running your own ministry or a member of a team. The action plan that follows can be modified to include or exclude action steps you believe are necessary or not needed.

To make things simple, we'll consider our end-of-the-year fundraising campaign that runs from August through January.

Keep in mind, each action item needs to be assigned a person responsible, the resources necessary, a deadline, and any budget costs.

Month 1

- Start working on the fundraising theme. Themes help donors catch the vision.
- Review last year's fundraising efforts – what worked, what didn't.

- Start brainstorming your goals early.
- Think about how you'll segment your donor audience—one message does not suit everyone.
- Consider which channels (newsletter, website, Facebook, email) you'll use to reach people.
- Take stock of the team member's skills, abilities and experiences. If you need help from outside the organization start looking early.

Month 2

- Review your fundraising materials (Facebook page, website, brochure) for accuracy—make sure everything is up to date and works flawlessly.
- Double-check the donation process by giving to yourself.
- Collect more stories and photos from those being helped to show how the organization is impacting those being helped.

Month 3

- Start to think about how and when your marketing pieces will go out (emails, newsletters, blog posts, Facebook ads).
- Consider ways advisory team members and major donors can help with the fundraising process.
- Create any campaign pieces – new brochure, donor card, "Thank You" emails.

Month 4

- Begin the testing phase by sending all the marketing pieces to team members for review.
- Correct any errors.
- Start sending out "warm-up" emails to potential donors.
- Begin thanking early donors.

Month 5

- Start making your phone calls.
- Grab coffee with your supporters and prospective donors.
- Start sending out your email appeals.
- Send out your "time is running out" emails at year's end.
- Continue to follow up with donors that have participated.
- Let donors know of your successes.

Month 6

- Make prospective donors aware of your successes.
- Thank everyone for their participation.
- Send out one last appeal—plenty of people miss deadlines.
- Do a postmortem to understand the lessons learned.

Stay flexible.

The 6-month schedule shown here, could be completed in less time. It's up to you to decide on how much to take on at one time.

Here are 6 Execution Takeaways to keep in mind:

<u>**6 Execution Takeaways:**</u>

1. Continue to cast the vision.
2. Stay on task.
3. Act quickly when things are not going well.
4. Shore up resources that are lacking.
5. Turn off what's not working and turn up what is.
6. Track the metrics that mean the most.

 **Find a Sample 6-month Fundraising Plan Schedule and First Quarter Worksheet at the end of this chapter.**

Ignite Your Fundraising

Sample 6-month Fundraising Plan Schedule

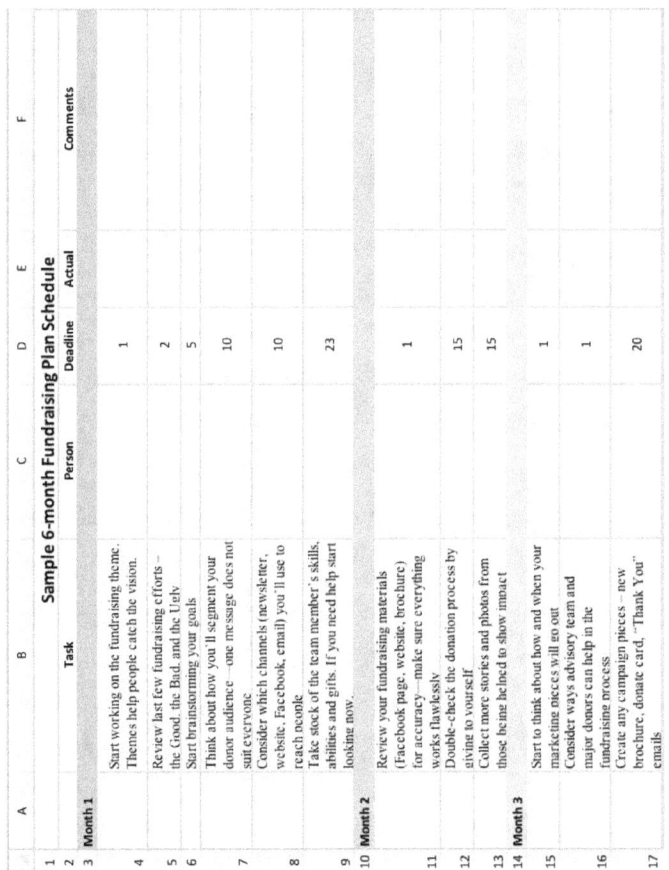

Download at:

ministrythrive.com/SampleFundraisingPlanSchedule.xlsx

Chapter 5/Setting Things in Motion

Ignite Your Fundraising

Sample 6-month Fundraising Plan Schedule

	A	B	C	D	E	F
1			Sample 6-month Fundraising Plan Schedule			
2		Task	Person	Deadline	Actual	Comments
3	**Month 4**					
4		Begin testing by sending all the marketing pieces to team members		1		
5		Correct any errors		5		
6		Start sending out warm-up emails to prospects and donors		10		
7		Begin thanking early donors		30		
8	**Month 5**					
9		Start making your phone calls		1		
10		Grab coffee with your prospects and donors		1		
11		Start sending out your email appeals		5		
12		Send out your "time is running out" emails		10		
13		Continue to follow up with donors that have participated		15		
14		Let other prospects and donors know of your successes		15		
15	**Month 6**					
16		Let other prospects and donors know of your successes		5		
17		Thank everyone for their participation		5		
18		Send out one last appeal—plenty of people miss deadlines		10		
19		Do a post mortem to understand the lessons learned		20		
20						

Download at:

ministrythrive.com/SampleFundraisingPlanSchedule.xlsx

Ignite Your Fundraising

Sample Fundraising Plan Worksheet

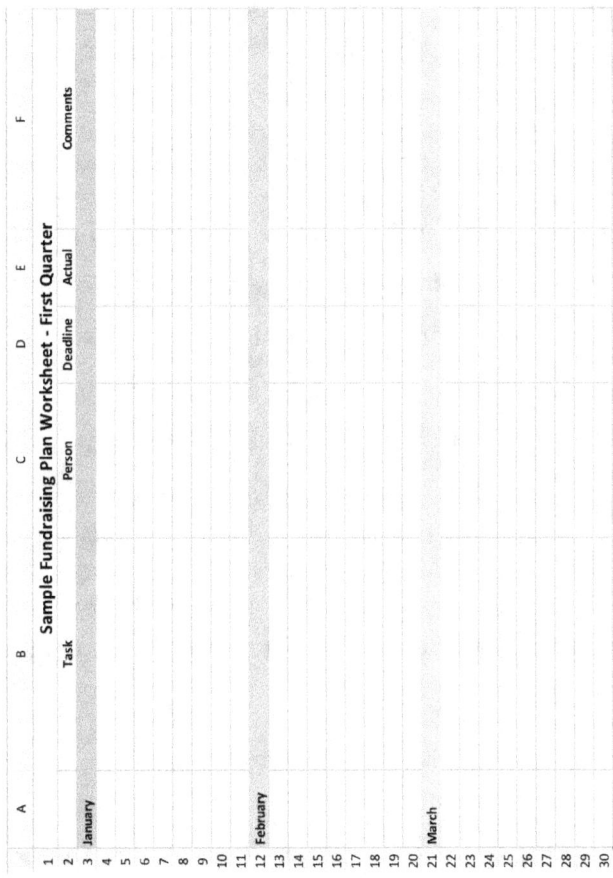

Download at:

ministrythrive.com/SampleFundraisingPlanWorksheet.xlsx

Chapter 5/Setting Things in Motion

Following Up

"It can take months to find a donor and mere moments to lose one." — Unknown

Before we dive into the follow up process, here is a sobering statistic that should drive us all to do better in following up with our donors and potential supporters:

19% of donors stop giving because of poor communication. (Stat courtesy of CauseVox)

Poor communication is not the only reason donors look for other opportunities to give. But, let's make sure our communication is anything but poor.

Let's divide our follow up discussion into two practices. First, we'll look at thanking people for their generosity, then talk about developing a stewardship plan to stay in touch with those that gave as well as educate, nurture, and engage the potential donor audience.

Being Grateful

Gratitude is not a feeling that should be dispensed because an email was received telling the organization a gift was received. There's more to gratitude than dropping "Thank You" cards in the US Mail or worse yet sending an automated email response—untouched by human hands.

Searching the web for "thanking donors" renders 21,000 entries. A few more than we can cover in this writing. Let's see if we can make several worthwhile generalizations:

Saying "Thank You" Should be Personal

Resist sending out a "canned" response after a person gives to your organization. The "thank you" should be personal. Of course, every donor cannot receive a uniquely different "thank you" effort can be expended to make the "thank you" look and sound like it's coming from a human being and not a machine.

Forget about a salutation that reads: Dear Donor, Valued Supporter, Ministry Friend, and so on. What could be more impersonal than not mentioning a person's name? Personalize each note by using the donor's first name if possible.

Forget about developing an email template to thank people. Use your standard email program without any bells and whistles. Remember, you're talking to a friend.

See gifts as the beginning of a beautiful relationship. Talk to your donors as you would family and friends. Pay as much attention to what they say as what it is you want said. Get to know who they are and what interests them most about what you're doing.

 **Think about thanking your donors for being who they are and not because they give. Send out 'Thank You" cards because you both share a common passion.**

Saying "Thank You" Should Take Time

The "Thank You" should take an amount of effort. Put thought into what you say to your donors. They have obviously thought about supporting your organization before making a gift.

The "Thank You" donors receive should show that you've put a measure of thought and effort into the process.

Remember, each interaction you have with your donors is another opportunity to share your passion. Strong donor relationships lead to lifelong support.

Saying "Thank You" should be meaningful to both parties.

Saying "Thank You" Should Express Authenticity

Don't mix a lot of jargon or business in the "Thank You." Keep it simple. It's hard to be authentic when using technology as it is.

Technology almost negates the personal touch when communicating with someone. It's hard to be personal when the recipient receives dozens if not hundreds of emails each week.

Send note cards. Not of the preprinted variety. Real, actual, hand-written notes.

Saying "Thank You" Should Convey Gratitude

Choose a board member or volunteer that truly enjoys the process of thanking people for their support. The person who has the gift of sharing appreciation. Ingratitude is hard to hide. People who go through the motions will be found out.

 **If you're having trouble writing your first "Thank You" letter. Check out the examples at: google.images.com and search for donor "thank you" letters.**

Not All Donors Are to be Treated Equal

A personalized "Thank You" card might go out to a family who supports the effort monthly with a $25 gift. However, if a person were to make a one-time major gift of say $1,000 or $2,000 that event deserves more attention. An immediate phone call (if possible) followed up by a personal note (not an email) or a visit expressing gratitude.

Donors can be thanked in a variety of ways. The possibilities are endless. Here are ideas:

- Send a handwritten note.
- Send an email.
- Make a phone call.
- Thank them in person.
- Post their names on your website and Facebook page.
- Send a small, meaningful gift.
- Profile your donors.
- Host a donor party.
- Offer a tour of your facility.
- Publically acknowledge their support.
- Send a video "Thank You".
- Involve recipients in the "Thank You" process.

Think about creating a tiered "Thank You" system where depending upon the amount given it causes a certain action on your team's part.

Ignite Your Fundraising

Avoid making mistakes in the process and send the "Thank You" out as soon as possible. Surely within 48 hours no matter what system you develop.

 **Find a Tiered "Thank You" System Sample and Worksheet at the end of this chapter.**

Keep the Spotlight on Those That Give

Thank donors for what their generosity has/or is accomplishing not what "the team" has done. Let the donors know specifically what their gifts have made happen.

Remember, without their generosity the organization would be at a standstill.

Be specific when sharing the impact. If possible, include stories by the recipients who are being affected. The more the impact is shared with photos the better.

Metrics or indicators are great ways to show progress. Have you ever seen the thermometer that has 75% colored in to show a non-profit's success on a project? Let donors know where you are.

Don't Send a "Thank You" Hinting at Another Gift

Send out the "Thank You" with no strings attached. Expect nothing in return. This is your opportunity to raise the donor's spirits and to let them know you value the relationship more than the gift.

Here are 6 "Thank You" Takeaways to keep in mind:

<u>**6 "Thank You" Takeaways:**</u>

1. Be human.
2. Don't treat every donor the same.
3. Invest time in saying "Thank You."
4. Be authentic.
5. Be prompt is saying "Thank You."
6. Keep the spotlight on the donor.

 Don't know how you'll find time to thank donors? Here's another good reason to form an advisory team.

Staying in Touch Beyond Saying "Thank You"

Let's briefly look over the ingredients of a stewardship plan, even though that topic belongs more in a discussion about donor relations and donor development, let's spend a few minutes here.

Most stewardship programs include these components:

An Accurate Donor File

You'll need to determine what donor information is required in the file to identify and communicate with each donor.

You'll need to appoint a person to watch over the donor file to keep things accurate and up to date.

You may want to segment the donors into groups, so communications can go out that are in line with their interests.

You may also want to store donor preferences on how they prefer to be contacted (by phone, email, US Mail).

Stewardship Defined

Time will need to be spent to define what "stewardship" means to your organization.

This definition should include the care and feeding and your donors:

- How and when will donors be acknowledged?
- What types of "Thank You" will be sent out and by what means?
- What regular communications will be sent to the donor?
- How will donor attrition/retention be tracked?

Goals of the Stewardship Program

For any program to be worthwhile there needs to be goals in place.

How will donor attrition be offset?

What level of donor retention is acceptable? How will that level be maintained and increased?

How will donors be encouraged to increase their level of commitment?

A Stewardship Program Budget

Will the program require outside staffing?

Will additional technology be needed?

How often will the program team report back?

The Stewardship Team

You'll need to make sure the team is made up of people that genuinely want to work with donors.

You'll need to make sure they have the necessary guidance, training and resources to be successful.

You'll need to ensure they understand the value of the program to the overall success of the organization.

Stewardship Communication Plan

You'll need to create a tiered "Thank You" System much like the one we discussed earlier.

Ignite Your Fundraising

Tiered "Thank You" System Sample

Gift	Action	Interval	Person
$25	Email	within 48 hours	
$50	"Thank You" card	within 48 hours	
$100	Thank You note from Project Manager	within 24 hours	
$500	Thank You call from Project Manager Small gift from recipient	Immediately	
$1,000	Thank You call from Board member Invitation to have lunch	Immediately	
Reocurring	"Thank You " card	within 48 hours	

Download at:

ministrythrive.com/TieredThankYouSystemSample.xlsx

Ignite Your Fundraising

Tiered "Thank You" System Worksheet

Download at:

ministrythrive.com/TieredThankYouSystemWorksheet.xlsx

Ignite Your Fundraising

Sample Follow Up Plan by Donor

Sample Follow Up Plan by Donor

This Sample Follow Up Plan By Donor covers proposed timelines for three donor situations: a one-time gift, monthly gifts, and major gifts received during the EOY campaign. After some period, perhaps 30 days, the donor's names should be moved over to the regular communication schedule that takes place during the year.

One-time Gift
Immediate
Tax deductible receipt sent by email.
Within 24 Hours
Personalized email thanking the person and highlight the gift's impact.
30 Days Out
Personalized email highlighting their gift and the project's impact.

Monthly Gift
Immediate
Tax deductible receipt sent by email.
Within 24 Hours
Phone call is possible thanking the person and highlight the gift's impact.
Monthly
Personalized email highlighting their gift and the project's impact and well as another donor's story on how supporting the project is changing their life.

Major Gift
Immediate
Tax deductible receipt sent by email.
Within 24 Hours
Phone call thanking the person and highlight the gift's impact.
Ongoing
Phone calls highlighting their gift and the project's impact. Follow up by email with details of the phone call.
Phone call telling another donor's story on how supporting the project is changing their life. Followed up by email with details of the phone call.

Copyright © 2018 ministryTHRIVE

Download at:

ministrythrive.com/SampleFollowUpPlanByDonor.pdf

Ignite Your Fundraising

Follow Up Plan by Donor Worksheet

Follow Up Plan by Donor Worksheet

Use this worksheet to cover the possible donor situations you'll incur. Decide what you'll do to follow up how and when. Change the response intervals to suit your needs.

One-time Gift

Immediate _____

Within 24 Hours _____

30 Days Out _____

Monthly Gift

Immediate _____

Within 24 Hours _____

Monthly _____

Major Gift

Immediate _____

Within 24 Hours _____

Continuous _____
_____
_____

Copyright © 2018 ministryTHRIVE

Download at:

ministrythrive.com/FollowUpPlanByDonorWorksheet.docx

Chapter 6/Following Up

Measuring Your Progress

"I've got a bad feeling about this." — Han Solo

Don't attempt to measure feelings or emotions—measure numbers.

What needs to be measured to show real success? Yes, we could look at the amount of funds being raised, but that won't tell us where we're having success and where we're likely wasting our fundraising resources and time.

If gifts are coming in, who's giving? What message is working best? What channel is showing the best results? It's important to make sure we're measuring the numbers that tell the actual story of what's taking place.

Let's say we send out 75 newsletters attached to emails. How will we know if people are opening the email and reading what we have written? They won't.

Ignite Your Fundraising

If these same emails are sent out through by way of an email marketing automation system such as MailChimp, which tracks opens and click-throughs, we'll know exactly how many are being read. If we send our emails out using a mail client such as Outlook or Apple's Mail program, we'll have no idea.

 MailChimp is a free service if you're emailing to fewer than 2,000 contacts and 12,000 emails per month.

So, how do we measure what?

Suppose we're reaching our donors and potential donors through a variety of channels, say: the website, support letters, newsletters, emails, social media, and face-to-face meetings. These avenues are not going to show the same success rates.

Let's spend a few moments drawing distinctions between what we'll call **vanity numbers** and **actionable metrics.** Vanity numbers might be the number of page views our website received last month or the number of "Likes" our Facebook page garnered this past week.

At first, we care about those numbers, but they're not the numbers we're after in the long run. We care most about the actions people take. Actions in the form of providing their email address, or other personal information, downloading our latest newsletter, or giving.

Chapter 7/Measuring Your Progress

Ignite Your Fundraising

 The three factors we care most about are *traffic*, *conversions*, and *average gift*. Those numbers tell the real story about our success to raise funds.

First, we need to generate **traffic**; the number of people being reached with our message. Next, those people must be compelled to take an action (**conversion**); say subscribing to our newsletter or donating to our cause. Last, we want to find ways to encourage those converts to be more involved; say by volunteering, giving more often or more regularly, or increasing their **average gift** size.

Let's breakdown the more popular ways we communicate with people and look at the numbers that really matter.

Face-to-face Meetings

Face-to-face meetings tend to be the most successful way to acquire new donors.

But, we'll have to do analysis and perform diagnostics on the actions and conversations that take place before we can determine our level of success.

Let's analyze a typical face-to-face meeting scenario.

When we ask people if we could meet, they are apt to respond in one of three ways: they'll say "yes", "no", or "now's not a good time."

Ignite Your Fundraising

What to do?

For the people that said "yes", our action is obvious—set up a time to meet.

What to do with those that said "no" and "now's not a good time?"

For the people that said "no" we could ask if they would support us in prayer. If they respond in a positive way, we could ask if they would not mind if we send them a few periodic emails to let them know how they could support the efforts on the ground.

For the people that said, "now's not a good time," they might mean now is not a good time or they may mean no. We won't know until we ask them a second or perhaps third question. The second question might be, "would a time next week work better for you?" If they say, "yes," we can book a time. Suppose they say next week is not good. Then perhaps they're trying to let us down easy, but are reluctant to say no. In that case, we revert to asking them to support us in prayer.

The same type of analysis and diagnostic exercises need to take place during the actual face-to-face meeting as well as afterwards.

We'll want to start developing meaningful metrics to determine if our face-to-face meetings are being profitable.

If we look across the many ways to communicate and engage people, there are dozens of metrics we could track. Let's keep things simple. Here are the face-to-face meeting metrics that are most important:

- How many appointment calls were made?
- How many people said, "yes", "no" and "now's not a good time?"
- How many "yes's" turned into actual meetings?
- How many "no's" are being followed up?
- How many "now's not a good time" turned into later meetings?
- How many new donors were acquired?
- What is the average gift?

With these numbers, we'll be able to tell if meeting potential donors is worth our investment of time.

It's important to know how many appointments we book each week or month. It's more telling how many of those people turn into donors. If we set 10 appointments per month and two of those people become donors, then it's easy to calculate that if we want the appointments to generate 5 new donors each month then we need to set 25 appointments per month. 5 appointments need to be set for each new donor that comes on board.

So, the number of appointments (**traffic** *per say*) becomes of secondary importance, while the number of people that say "yes" (**conversions**) is our primary goal. We're also interested in what people give. If the 5 new donors gifted $500 together, then the **average gift** is $100.

If 25 appointments per month is an unrealistic number, then it becomes obvious we need to look to other avenues to help generate the number of new donors we need to acquire during our fundraising campaign.

This same type of analysis and diagnostics needs to take place with each form of communication we use.

 Don't add people to your email list without asking their permission.

Websites

It's good to understand that not only humans visit websites. Bots, or computer programs, make up 52% of all Internet traffic. There are good bots and not so good bots. Google bots, are good bots. Google sends bots to all websites to see if there have been updates made to the web pages recently.

Charlatans from countries outside (and inside) the US send bad bots to websites to scrape email addresses to send back SPAM.

Let's say 100 visitors came to your website last week. There is a good chance that more than half of those visitors were not human.

The first order of business for a website owner is to create **traffic** opportunities. Once the right traffic is flowing to the site, the next step in the process is to encourage that traffic to take a specific action (**conversion**), say watching video, subscribing to a newsletter, or giving (**average gift**).

Don't believe the phrase, "If you build it they will come." They won't. There is so much noise on the Internet that the small fish in this gigantic ocean have little chance of attracting the right audience without budgeting a significant amount of money.

Here's an example:

Say you are supporting an orphanage on the African continent. There are 347,000 pages dealing with "orphans in Africa." Knowing that, let's further propose that you want to attract donors that are looking to support orphans in Ghana. If you search for "supporting orphans Ghana" in Google you'll find over 337,000 pages. Your website needs to be listed in the first three to five positions if there is any hope the person searching will find your website.

Traffic to a website is good. Conversions from that traffic are best.

Here are 6 Website Takeaways to keep in mind:

6 Website Takeaways:

1. Make the site easy to read on mobile devices.
2. Have an obvious value proposition and call to action.
3. Current, compelling, relevant copy.
4. Talk about the impact being made.
5. List how the funds are spent.
6. **Have a friend check the spelling and grammar.**

So how should the website initially be used to convert potential donors?

In smaller organizations, websites should be used to add legitimacy to the project and to extend the conversation that takes place after the first meeting. Say you have an appointment and tell the person you met with to check out the website where they can find out more about what's happening. The website extents the conversation.

Brochures can only tell so much of the story. Besides, brochures cannot be updated every time newsworthy events happen. Blogs on the other hand can be updated moment by moment and are a great storytelling tool to drive potential donors to the website.

 Of course, nothing will ever replace face-to-face meetings as the most effective way to close.

Support Letters

If support letters are sent by US Mail, there is no way to tell if the right people are opening or read what's been sent. The only indication we'll have of the letter's success is if an addressee responds back perhaps with an email or a gift.

If you prefer to send out support letters by mail, then send an email out announcing the letter is on its way and then follow up with a second email to ensure the person received your communique.

When they reply, you can track the letter's arrival (**traffic**), if they give (**conversion**) and the size of their gift (**average gift**).

If 100 support letters are sent out and the average number of people who support the organization is 3, then the conversion rate for sending out the support letters is 3%. If the amount given by the 3 people is $150 then the average gift size if $50.

Remember, a good response rate from support letters is less than 5%.

If constituents are used to hearing from you on a regular basis and the newsletters are relevant and interesting, then the open rate will go up. Regular does not mean once a year. Think more like monthly or bimonthly.

Here are 6 Support Letter Takeaways to keep in mind:

6 Support Letter Takeaways:

1. Share your passion.
2. List the challenges you face.
3. Talk about the impact being made and the urgency of the need.
4. Focus on the donor not the organization.
5. Give the donor giving options.
6. **Have a friend check your spelling and grammar.**

Newsletters

It's best to send newsletters out using an email marketing system such as MailChimp for the same reasons we covered earlier. There's no way to tell what's happening at the other end if you're using US Mail. A MailChimp-like program would be the only way to track the opens to see if people are opening the email that contains your news.

The only way to know if your newsletter efforts are paying off (**conversions**) is to ask the reader to take an action; visit your website, "like" your Facebook page, or by giving (**average gift**).

Newsletters are notorious thieves of time and resources. It's important to know if the newsletter is having a positive effect on your prospective donors or donors. Is what you're writing about provoking them to take some action?

If not, stop publishing. Try another engagement activity.

Here are 6 Newsletter Takeaways to keep in mind:

6 Newsletter Takeaways:

1. Make sure the information is "newsworthy."
2. Have consistent publication dates.
3. Skip the templates and go for great content instead.
4. Share your passion.
5. Talk about the impact being made and the urgency of the need.
6. **Have a friend check your spelling and grammar.**

Emails

CauseVox has published interesting stats on non-profits sending out emails.

- **12%** of emails sent are considered spam because the recipient does not have the sender's email address in their address book.
- **25.96%** of non-profit emails are opened. The industry rate is only 6%.
- Having social media icons within the email increases click-through rates by as much as **158%**.
- Personalization increases the click-through rate by **14%**.
- **53%** of emails are opened on mobile devices.

Ignite Your Fundraising

- Sending out **4** emails a month as opposed to 1 increases click-through rates.

Here are a few more statistics from ConstantContact, another email marketing automation company much like MailChimp:

- Non-profits average a 20% open rate for their emails with a click-through rate of 8%. The average conversion rate of that 8% is between 1.5 and 3.5%.

Let's run a few test numbers using these percentages.

Say we send out 1,000 emails. That means that, on average, 200 people (20%) will open the email. If only 8% of that 200 people, click-through to the donation page our number now drops to 16. Let's be generous and say 5% of the people do donate, that's less than one person of out 1,000 potential donors.
Don't be discouraged.

Open, click-through, and conversion rates can improve exponentially by being consistent in sending the emails out on a regular basis, so people expect to hear from you, and by making sure the content is relevant to the reader, is impactful, shows progress, and has calls to action that are clear and concise.

If we improved the open rate to 50% and the click-through and conversion rates by 20% and 15% the donation picture would change dramatically. Out of the 1,000 emails sent now 500 people open what we've sent. 100 people would be clicking-through, and 15 people would be donating.

These rates would continue to improve the more we sharpen our message and approach. Don't lose heart.

Here are 6 Email Takeaways to keep in mind:

<u>**6 Email Takeaways:**</u>

1. Resist using a template.
2. Personalize the salutation.
3. Use compelling Subject lines.
4. Talk about the impact being made and the urgency of the need.
5. **Have a friend check your spelling and grammar.**
6. Remember, you're writing to a friend.

Social Media

Let's look at Facebook for instance. The number of friends and followers we have and the number of "likes" our stories receive tell us about our **traffic** to the Facebook page. These numbers do signal a conversion of sorts, but not the conversion number we're most interested in seeing. We're more interested in people who visit our website from the Facebook page (**conversion**) to gain a better understanding of what we're trying to accomplish and give (**average**

Ignite Your Fundraising

gift) once at our site. These are the conversion numbers that are significant.

If our Facebook page receives 50 new "likes" per month and 5 of those people, click through to our website and donate then we could say our conversion rate from Facebook "likes" is 10%.

 **Please don't think we're saying numbers are all that is important. But, we can't tell we're getting closer to our destination unless we take notice of the number of miles traveled. Numbers tell the amount of progress being made. Numbers tell the real story.**

Here are 6 Social Media Takeaways to keep in mind:

6 Social Media Takeaways:

1. Engage.
2. Interact and be human.
3. Being social is a two-way street.
4. Stick with your brand's voice.
5. Keep your profile current.
6. If conversions are NOT happening—stop what you're doing.

 **Find a Measuring Your Progress Worksheet at the end of this chapter.**

Ignite Your Fundraising

The Measuring Your Progress spreadsheet helps track from where the gifts are coming. We could also add email addresses to this table and track those as well.

It's important to know where we're making the most progress, so we can divert more resources toward that effort.

You may be surprised at which communication method shows the best results—be flexible and stay open-minded. Be ready to act on the information.

Ignite Your Fundraising

Measuring Your Progress Worksheet

Download at:

ministrythrive.com/MeasuringYourProgressWorksheet.xlsx

EIGHT

Getting Better Results

"I coulda been a contender" — Terry Malloy,
On the Waterfront, 1954

Getting better results is a process that should be underway continuously—while the fundraising campaign is underway.

This section can also double as a postmortem outline so that a "lessons learned" exercise can take place to improve the fundraising results next time.

In this section, we'll consider 241 questions to ensure the fundraising energies going forward are well spent and that they help us become better fundraisers.

Sending out the same support letter twice in the month of December, after not communicating with donors during the year, will not produce the desired results. We've all heard the quote on what insanity is:

> *"Doing the same thing over and over expecting different results."*— Unknown

Unfortunately, in certain fundraiser's minds they expect better results the second time they send out the same publication.

 You can't improve what's not being tracked and measured.

To refine and improve our results, we'll have to be tracking the numbers that tell us where our fundraising measures are working and where they need shoring up.

For instance, we can't send out a newsletter during October, November and December, thinking surely the readers will notice our website link at the bottom of the page, immediately understand our financial situation, and head to the donate page on our website and give generously. Has that happened to you recently?

So where to start the "getting better results" discussion?

We need to disassemble our EOY fundraising approach into its discrete components, so we can examine each one individually to see where improvements can be achieved. Or if shortcomings can be removed or replaced.

Each of the following sections here coincide with the seven previous chapters we've covered together.

First, you'll find a series of questions to ponder followed by suggestions you may want to consider using if they seem to apply to your situation.

 **There is no Fundraising Silver Bullet or So-many-step Plan that works flawlessly for every non-profit. Each organization needs to develop what works best for them.**

The questions need answering by each fundraiser individually. What works for one organization may not work for another.

We all have varying goals, donors, stories to tell, messaging, timing, communication methods, team members, and skills.

Now, let's look at the discrete parts of our fundraising approach to see where fine-tuning might help us achieve better results:

 Numbers remove the emotions and tell the real story.

Deciding on Your Fundraising Goals

- ***Were the goals motivating?*** If there is a goal that the team has not fully gotten behind, is there a way the goal can be revised or redefined, so people better understand the objective? Were the goals in line with our mission?
- ***Did any of the goals end up not being specific, measurable, attainable, relevant, or time bound?*** If there is a goal that fell short of the SMART system can it be reshaped to better meet the criteria?
- ***Were the goals written down?*** If the goals were not recorded, make a second attempt to keep things noted. Having the goals written down helps keep everyone focused on the prize and keeps everyone heading in the same direction.
- ***Did the fundraising effort stray from the original goals?*** If some scope creep was experienced, are there ways to recover or rein in the objectives to get back on track?
- ***Did the campaign objectives suit the donors being approached?*** If there was any misalignment between the campaign goals and the donors, are there ways to recover?
- ***Were any goals we shortsighted?*** Can any of the goals be sharpened or broadened to capture a larger audience? It's important the fundraising campaign reach potential donors.

Let's suppose after having a discussion on goal setting, the objectives were on mission, motivating, specific, attainable, measurable, relevant, and the deadlines were reasonable. If that's the case,

Ignite Your Fundraising

perhaps the reason or reasons the fundraising efforts fell short lie elsewhere.

Acquiring New Donors

Acquiring new potential donors is always one of the most challenging parts of any fundraising campaign aside from reaching the financial goal.

- ***Were 100 people identified?*** If 100 names were not achieved, were others approached jog one's memory to see if there were missing names? If there were people that were not contacted, were they dropped from the list? If so, perhaps another attempt should be made to contact them.
- ***Was everyone reachable?*** Were realistic goals set on reaching a certain number of people each week? Were the numbers met? If not, why not?
- ***How did the appointment process go?*** What was the success rate on acquiring new donors? Are there changes that could be made to make the appointment process more successful? Could a trusted friend critique the appointment process to give more insight on how to improve things? Was information always left behind and was there follow up? Were people's questions answered? Were they tracked if they visited the website afterwards?
- ***Were the efforts successful in contacting people whom you did not know?*** This can be a trying process to get started.

Were donors asked for referrals? Were the small gatherings effective? If not, why not? Were there formats that worked better than others? Did the family or friend group produce better results? Did delaying "the ask" work well? Were they tracked if they visited the website afterwards?

- **Were you able to reach people groups who did not know about your organization?** Did a trusted friend appraise the presentation and offer ways to improve it? Did one small group produce better results than the rest? Did the timing and locations work well? Were ways explored to get the messages out beyond the website or Facebook page—speak at local events or to business groups, write guest posts, find ways to raise the visibility of your organization beyond your reach?

Telling a Great Story

It will be hard to get honest answers to some of these observations if the stories were not read by a few trusted associates before being sent out. The writer cannot act as an impartial editor or reviewer.

 It would also be helpful if a few trusted donor's comments were solicited.

- **Did every story have a purpose?** Was the purpose of each story clear and concise? If not, it will likely not be clear in anyone else's mind who reads the piece.

- **Were hooks employed to grab the reader's attention?** Did the first sentence grab the reader's attention? There are loads of examples across the Internet—use Google. Get out of the habit of working in a vacuum.
- **Was the reader drawn into the story as soon as possible?** Did the first few sentences immediately draw the reader into the story? Did you tell the reader where you were taking them?
- **Did you wander?** Be honest here. Was too much talked about? Could you have said less and still made the story great?

   In storytelling, less is more.

- **Were you able to keep it real by using photos and exact details?** If "hero" photos and details were not available this time, what's the plan for the next fundraising campaign? Think of using stock photos from the same area and replace them over time as the ones needed are acquired. Don't let a single photo squander a fundraising campaign opportunity.
- **Did we hit one out of the park tapping into donor emotions?** The proof here will be whether gifts were made. You need to find out. If not, why not? Again, ask a trusted backer.
- **Could donors see themselves in the story?** Here's a second indication that will be verified by gifts. Don't get too far in the weeds when telling the story. Drop the jargon and vocabulary people are not familiar with reading.

Ignite Your Fundraising

- ***Were you able to bring in those being affected?*** Were recipients brought into the stories? If not, was there a backup plan? Communication tools such as SKPYE help close the gap when dealing with locations around the globe. Did the pictures and dialogue help tell the story?

Getting Your Message Out

This section deals with how the message is packaged and the channels being used to communicate the information.

Fundraising—it's not only about the money. It's about offering people the opportunity to be involved in what God's doing. It's about the prospect of speaking for people who cannot speak for themselves—who cannot be sitting comfortably, enjoying a cup of coffee or herbal tea with the prospective donor.

- ***Did donors understand the purpose in raising the funds?*** Did they grasp the urgency? Were they assured their gifts would be spent wisely? Could they see the benefits their gift would create for the recipients? Did they realize the importance of their participation? Did they feel all their questions were answered? Did they understand the suffering that would continue if the projected funds did not come in?
- ***Was sharing the past successes of the organization effective?*** Were you able to share the impact of the

organization in "real" terms? Could you show that lives were better off, there was less disease, families were experiencing a better quality of life, lives were being saved, children were safer, and people were entering God's Kingdom? Donors need to see positive, practical, life-changing results.

- **Did sharing the future direction excite donors?** Did donors see the organization's future as more exciting, impactful, and far-reaching? Was the organization able to express their vision in "future-terms?" Did the path forward make sense in the mind of the supporters? Did they see the projects and timing as practical and realistic?

- **Was the messaging aligned with the mission statement?** Alignment is everything when it comes to the success of a strategy no matter what the cause. Here are a few statistics that could cause one to lose heart – but know that God is in charge:

65% of organizations have an agreed-upon strategy

14% of employees understand the strategy

10% +/- of organizations successfully execute the strategy

Forbes.com

Is the organization's mission statement clear, concise, and understood? Is it easy for donors to see how the fundraising efforts connect with and compliment the mission? Was it easy for donors to see how the fundraising campaign connected with the mission?

Ignite Your Fundraising

- **Was the use of SKYPE effective?** Were technologies such as: SKYPE, GoToMeeting, Voca, oovoo, and WhatsApp used to close the geographic gap when communicating with prospective donors and supporters? Were there other technologies that need exploring for future campaigns? Was information sent out after the conversations to recap what was discussed and to help educate those unfamiliar with the organization?

- **How many in-person visits took place each month?** Were face-to-face meetings leveraged as much as Possible? What was the success rate of acquiring potential donors? Were the handouts effective in educating people about the causes the organization is fighting? Are there ways the face-to-face strategy could be improved?

- **How many emails were sent out, to who and when?** Was a marketing automation system such as MailChimp or ConstantContact used to send out and monitor the emails? Were the emails sent out consistently and on time? Were follow up techniques in place to answer people's questions? Did the number of emails that went out seem sufficient? Were the unsubscribes low? Did prospective donors appreciate the use of communicating by email? Were other communication channels suggested? Were the emails personalized?

- **How many phone conversations took place?** Were the phone conversations fruitful? Was the time well spent? Did this seem to be a good way to communicate?

- **Did we have all the necessary marketing materials?** Do the marketing materials (logo, business card, brochure, handouts) have a professional appearance? Did they carry the message well? Were special end-of-the-year materials created? Was everything accurate and up-to-date?
- **Was the theme welcomed?** Was a theme employed? Did the theme attract attention? Did the staff rally around the theme? Was the theme in line with the mission? Did the theme end up being a powerful motivator? Did it raise awareness of the organization and its cause?
- **Were there communication channels that were not used, underused or not explored?** Did the staff have the necessary skills to use the latest technologies? Were communications not exploited even though it was apparent potential donors and supporters were present? Will other channels be looked at in the future? Is training needed to take advantage of the latest technologies? Were the channels used with raising funds in mind or advertising the organization and not used to build relationships first?

Setting Things in Motion

Aside from the planning stage the execution of the plan is probably the next hardest component of any successful fundraising campaign. If we take a step back and look at a simple action plan, it includes: the goals to be achieved, the people involved, the resources necessary, the skills employed, the timing, and the metrics to be measured.

Let's consider each of the elements:
- **Were the goals clear and concise?** - Did every team member understand the campaign objectives? Was their support obvious? Was there a lack of focus? Did competing goals surface while the campaign was underway that distracted the team?
- **Were the right people picked for the project?** *Did they have the correct skills? Were people available when needed? Did they believe they had the necessary support and leadership from management? Did everyone understand their role?* Was there an unwillingness to change? Did any team members feel unnecessarily burdened?
- **Were the proper resources available?** – If materials were needed were they up to date and available (website, newsletters, blog posts, emails, donor cards, "Thank You" materials?) Did everyone understand their use? Was follow through present?
- **Did the skills employed leave some staff behind or unprepared**? – *Was any training needed? Were people uncomfortable using the technologies? Did the assigned tasks complement each person's skills?*
- **Did the timing make sense?** – Was there a loss of momentum? Were there disruptions that caused delays? Was too much expected of team members?

- **The metrics to be measured** – Were the right metrics followed? Was there failure to celebrate success? Was reality ignored? Was change resisted? Was the team flexible?

Following Up

There are literally many dozens of ways to thank donors listed on the Internet. The questions in this section helps one sharpen the "Thank You" process.

- ***Was being grateful difficult to pull off?*** Were you able to appoint a team member to follow up on thanking donors? Are the "Thank Yous" being tracked? (This may be another good reason to form an advisory team or at a minimum to develop a fundraising committee.)
- ***Were the "Thank Yous" Personal?*** Were the emails personalized? Was the tone less formal and more personal? Was the email structured more like a human was responding and less like a canned reply? Was the closing from a human and not an organization?
- ***Did you decide to skip the email template?*** Did you drop the email template and go with a text-only format?
- ***Do you have a process in place to thank people even when they don't give?*** Have you thought of sending out thank yous to people for just listening, for their faithfulness and consideration?
- ***Are you taking time to say, "Thank You"?*** Is the current

"Thank You" process mechanical and unemotional? Is the process seen as something that takes up valuable time that could be used elsewhere?

- **Was authenticity expressed during the "Thank You" process?** Do the donors understand how their support enriches the lives of those being helped? Were feelings of gratitude shared in a truly meaningful way?
- **Were you able to express honest gratitude during the "Thank You" process**? It's important that donors are more than a financial resource; use them as a sounding board or for advice. Were you able to find ways to express your gratitude?
- **Was a system put in place that differentiated donors based on the size of their gift?** Is that system manageable?
- **Have you found creative ways to keep the spotlight on those that give?** Are the donors being made to feel as though their contributions are making all the difference? Were handwritten notes sent? Did you take the time to thank them in person? Would it make sense to post their names on the website or Facebook page? Was a small, meaningful gift sent? Were donors profiled in a newsletter? Was hosting a donor party feasible? Did touring the facility make sense? Were there ways to publically acknowledge their support? Was a "Thank You" video sent? Were you able to involve recipients in the "Thank You" process?
- **Did you develop a policy whereby donors are thanked without hinting at another gift?** Is that a policy you could adopt?

Measuring Your Progress

Measuring our progress will be difficult, if not impossible, if we haven't taken the time to compile meaningful statistics. We'll want to keep an eye on the **traffic, conversions,** and **average gifts** that were generated from the donation page on your website, your support letters, emails, social media efforts, and face-to-face meetings.

Without good metrics to study, where we were successful and where we could have done better will be elusive.

Here are questions to think over:

- ***Did we raise the projected funds?*** This figure, of course, is the final determining factor in our success in our efforts to raise the needed end-of-the-year funds. How close did we get? Did we do better than last year?
- ***Was GivingTuesday a success?*** If GivingTuesday was instituted, was is well received? Did donors see it as "another ask" or was the day celebrated? Are there ways to make the announcement leading up to the day, or the day itself, better? What can we learn from other organizations that have had more success with GivingTuesday?
- ***Was including current donors and advisory team members successful?*** Did the peer-to-peer fundraising work well? Did they think the support from the organization was satisfactory and did they have everything they needed? Were the donors

surveyed to see how the system might be improved?

- **Was the budget workable?** There are non-profits which resist spending money on marketing when raising funds. If that's your position, did you seek people to underwrite the effort so that all the gifts that were donated went to the work on the ground? If more money were available, could added success have been gained? Are there places were money could have been saved or appropriated elsewhere?

- **Were there any areas where people were burning out or overwhelmed?** Were the team members well-matched to their tasks? If you were the only one working on the fundraising, is it time to form an advisory team to get the necessary help? Will training take place during the coming year to better prepare people for later fundraising? Do additional resources need to be secured to ensure success?

- **Are there places where we can eliminate wasted effort or resources?** If we take a step back from the fundraising process and look with an objective eye, are there places where the year-end endeavor can be shored up or streamlined? Did we have a "Plan B" in place when things or staff were unable to handle the load? Were there unnecessary time delays? Were any parts of the fundraising process over-engineered or over managed, or too complicated for the team members? Was time wasted doing what needed to be done a second time?

 "The most dangerous kind of waste is the waste we do not recognize" **Shigeo Shingo, Toyota**

- ***Were there things that were not anticipated?*** If gifts failed to come in did, we change the strategy or stay the course? If team members were absent or failed to complete their portion of the tasks, did we overburden the remaining members or look to enlist help from others? Were we able to anticipate problems before they arose and became serious? Did we mitigate their impact? Did team members step-up and take control?
- ***Are there places we can donate more time or effort?*** As we reflect on our progress or success, are there places next year where we'll donate more time, resources, and energy? Do we need to start the end-of-the-year fundraising process earlier next year? Are there marketing materials (update website, blog, social media, brochure, et al.) that need refining?
- ***Are there skills we could add to produce better results?*** If we didn't blog or use social media this year, will we employ the technology in future fundraising campaigns? Do we need to consider taking advantage of additional fundraising educational opportunities? If oversight of the moving parts of the campaign were challenging, are there management techniques we could learn? If storytelling was difficult, how will we improve the process next time?
- ***Are there ways we can reduce or eliminate disruptions?*** Did fuzzy goals or poor communication cause disruption? Was "scope creep" an issue? Is more management needed? Is more oversight necessary? Is more preparation in order? Was a helpful, positive attitude always present?

Don't rush the process in looking over these questions. Take the time each section deserves to gain the most understanding.

Don't lose the end-of-the-year fundraising momentum.

When a baseball player knocks the ball out of the park. He doesn't drop his bat at home plate and walk back to the dugout. He rounds the bases to score the run. He's not only paid to hit, he's paid to score runs.

Why settle for good results when great results might be just around the corner? Why not use the New Year to crank up those tactics you were unsure of or left behind when the campaign started to see if your intuition was right or wrong?

Don't be afraid of too much success. If you have a winning strategy squeeze every opportunity out of it you can. Great fundraising plans unfortunately have a short lifecycle.

Use the end-of-the-year as a beginning point not an ending.

Blessings when executing your next fundraising campaign.

 **Find a Getting Better Results Worksheet at the end of this chapter.**

Ignite Your Fundraising

Getting Better Results Worksheet

Getting Better Results Worksheet

Don't rush the process in looking over these questions. Take the time each section deserves to gain the most understanding.

Deciding on Your Fundraising Goals

_____
_____
_____
_____

Acquiring New Prospective Donors and Donors

_____
_____
_____
_____

Telling a Great Story

_____
_____
_____
_____

Copyright © 2018 ministryTHRIVE

Download at:

ministrythrive.com/GettingBetterResultsWorksheet.docx

Getting Better Results Worksheet

Getting Your Message Out

Setting Things in Motion

Following Up

Measuring Your Success

Copyright © 2018 ministryTHRIVE

Download at:

ministrythrive.com/GetterBetterResultsWorksheet.docx

NINE

End-of-the-year Fundraising

"No one has ever become poor by giving." — Anne Frank

Raising funds at the end of the year is not much different than an organization's normal yearlong fundraising effort—just on a more compressed schedule.

EOY Communication Differs

How should our end-of-the-year communications differ from the normal course of conversation:

- You may want to elaborate more when sharing end-of-the-year statistics on the organization's successes.
- You may want to share statistics on what makes the EOY such a great time to give.
- You may want to bring prospective donors and supporters up to speed on the challenges the organization still faces and

hopes to eliminate in the coming year.
- You may want to send out more than the normal string of one or two emails per year.
- You may want to spend more time thanking people for their generous support over the past year.
- You may want to try and reach people through a different channel, say social media, if you are not using that platform on a normal basis.
- You may want to highlight your various giving options to let people know there are choices they may not be aware of.
- You may want to leave "the ask" out of a few emails sent during November and December even though this may sound a little like heresy.
- You may want to be blatantly honest with your supporters if you find yourself in financial trouble.
- You may want to introduce the idea of having your most faithful donors engage in peer-to-peer fundraising.
- You may want to try introducing GivingTuesday as a means of generating additional funds. Many non-profits have set the Tuesday after Thanksgiving aside as GivingTuesday.

End-of-the-year fundraising activities such as the planning process usually starts around August with things ramping up in November and peaking in December.

Organizations look to raise funds at year's end for three main reasons: it makes sense to leverage the generosity window that exists at the end of the year. People are more giving during the holiday season. Second, organizations look to replenish budget deficits that may exist as the year comes to a close. And last, ministries may be looking to fund a special project they have eyed all year but have been unable to get funded.

From the donor's perspective, the holiday season is a great time to think of others and not just themselves. And second, giving to offset a tax liability as the result of a fruitful year makes sense.

All great reasons to participate on both sides.

End-of-the-year fundraising includes the same steps as the yearlong process: setting goals, acquiring new donors, telling a great story, getting your message out, executing things well, following up, measuring your progress, and tweaking tactics for the best results.

End-of-the-year fundraising is something anyone, including YOU, can do and be darn successful at it. It may seem like a scary process at first. The funding activity takes planning, preparation, patience, persistence, and a good dose of perspiration.

Use **Ignite Your Fundraising** as a guide to develop a strong, year-long fundraising strategy or apply it as a guidebook to develop and execute a fundraising strategy that successfully closes the year-end financial gap—the choice is up to you.

Ignite Your Fundraising

> *"Whatever the motivation, charities receive between 40% to 70% of their annual contributions in the five-week window leading up to year's end. Some organizations receive upwards of 30% in the last three days."* – courtesy of Abila Inc.

During the end-of-the-year fundraising period you may want to suspend your normal communication and engagement processes during November and December to focus more on your EOY message.

 Make sure to create a sense of urgency as the year ends.

 **Find a Sample EOY Fundraising Plan Schedule, and Worksheet at the end of this chapter.**

Ignite Your Fundraising

Sample EOY Fundraising Plan Schedule

	Task	Person	Deadline	Actual	Comments
August					
	Start working on the fundraising theme. Themes help people catch the vision.		1		
	Review last year's EOY fundraising effort – the Good, the Bad, and the Ugly		2		
	Start brainstorming your goals		5		
	Think about how you'll segment your donor audience—one message does not suit everyone		10		
	Consider which channels (newsletter, website, Facebook, email) you'll use to reach people		10		
	Take stock of the team member's skills, abilities and gifts. If you need help start looking now.		23		
September					
	Review your fundraising materials (Facebook page, website, brochure) for accuracy—make sure everything works flawlessly		1		
	Double-check the donation process by giving to yourself		15		
	Collect more stories and photos from those being helped to show impact		15		
October					
	Start to think about how and when your marketing pieces will go out		1		
	Consider ways advisory team and major donors can help in the fundraising process		1		
	Decide if GivingTuesday will play a role in this year's fundraising		1		
	Create any campaign pieces – new brochure, donate card, "Thank You" emails		20		

Download at:

ministrythrive.com/SampleEOYFundraisingPlanSchedule.xlsx

Ignite Your Fundraising

Sample EOY Fundraising Plan Schedule

	A	B	C	D	E	F
19	**November**					
20		Begin testing by sending all the marketing pieces to team members		1		
21		Correct any errors		5		
22		Start sending out warm-up EOY emails to prospects and donors		10		
23		Send out GivingTuesday announcements		20		
24		Send out/post GivingTuesday materials		20		
25		Begin thanking early donors		30		
26	**December**					
27		Start making your phone calls		1		
28		Grab coffee with your prospects and donors		1		
29		Start sending out your email appeals		5		
30		Send out your "time is running out" emails at year's end		10		
31		Continue to follow up with donors that have participated		15		
32		Let other prospects and donors know of your successes		15		
33	**January**					
34		Let other prospects and donors know of your successes		5		
35		Thank everyone for their participation		5		
36		Send out one last appeal—plenty of people miss deadlines		10		
37		Do a post mortem to understand the lessons learned		20		

Download at:

ministrythrive.com/SamleEOYFundraisingPlanSchedule.xlsx

Ignite Your Fundraising

Sample EOY Fundraising Plan Worksheet

Download at:

ministrythrive.com/SampleEOYFundraisingPlanWorksheet.xlsx

Ignite Your Fundraising

About the Author

John founded ministryTHRIVE in 2018. It's mission: **Provide exceptional online learning experiences to ensure those in ministry master the skills necessary to achieve their goals.**

Before ministryTHRIVE, John founded InPlainSite Marketing, a leader in developing and delivering digital marketing strategies. John consulted and presented to Fortune 100 and 500 companies. He is a bestselling author of sixteen books. John's musings are regularly picked up by TheStreet.com, Entrepreneur.com, Visa Business, *Yahoo! Finance*, MSNBC.com, The Globe and Mail, Reuters, and The New York Daily News.

John has served on the boards of nonprofits for more than a dozen years. He has enjoyed leading as either president, chairman of the board or as a director doing what he can to help organizations succeed. He has also valued his time as a volunteer in the trenches.

As president and chairman of the board, John has helped launch a crisis pregnancy center and thrift shop while living in Illinois. In Colorado, he was asked to be president and chairman of the board for a startup Christian school in Woodland Park. He has also served as a director on the board of an entrepreneurial organization, Middle Market Entrepreneurs, in Colorado Springs. He has served on a leadership council, as creative director and as a church volunteer in many other capacities. John believes his most rewarding times as a volunteer are when he gets to work alongside Kay or one of their children or grandchildren. Today, John's life centers on God, family, church, and community.

John loves spending time with Kay, his bride and best friend of 48 years of marriage. They have three of the greatest kids, okay grownups, on this planet as well as eight grandchildren. John and Kay live in Colorado.

BY
JOHN D. LEAVY

ALSO FROM THE IGNITION SERIES:

*Ignite Your
Donor Passion*

Available at Amazon.com
or wherever books are sold.

....

Find more great resources at ministrythrive.com.

www.ingramcontent.com/pod-product-compliance
Lightning Source LLC
Chambersburg PA
CBHW052303220526
45471CB00001B/469